T0287979

The Resilient Founder

The Resilient Founder

THE RESILIENT FOUNDER

LESSONS IN ENDURANCE FROM STARTUP ENTREPRENEURS

Mahendra Ramsinghani

WILEY

For general information on our other products and services or for technical support, please contact our Customer Care Department within the United States at (800) 762-2974, outside the United States at (317) 572-3993 or fax (317) 572-4002.

Wiley also publishes its books in a variety of electronic formats. Some content that appears in print may not be available in electronic formats. For more information about Wiley products, visit our web site at www.wiley.com.

Library of Congress Cataloging-in-Publication Data is Available:

ISBN 9781119839736 (Hardback)
ISBN 9781119839750 (ePDF)
ISBN 9781119839743 (ePub)

Cover Design: Wiley
Cover Image: © Bobbie Carlyle, Sculptor

SKY10031473_111821

In memory of minds afire

Austen Heinz, Aaron Swartz, Jody Sherman
Sreeram Veerangandham,
and many more . . .

This book is dedicated to
that indomitable spirit in every founder
that respects the darkness
and brings light
for a better future for all.

A book should serve as the axe for the frozen sea within us.
— *Franz Kafka*

Table of Discontents

Table of Discontents

Foreword

Brad Feld

I had my first major depressive episode as an adult in 1990. At the time, I was running my first company, Feld Technologies, which was going well. However, my work on a PhD program at MIT was not, and I dropped out of the program. At the same time, my first marriage imploded for various reasons, including my extreme focus on work. And, while Feld Technologies was succeeding, I was exhausted and bored with the actual work.

My experience of depression is the complete absence of joy. I'm functional and can do my work, but it takes all of my energy to get out of bed, get out of the house, make it through eight hours, and get back home. In the evenings, I don't have an interest in anything – food, reading, TV, sex, or exercise. Instead, I sit in the bathtub or lie in bed and stare at the ceiling, eventually falling asleep.

This depressive episode lasted two years. I did therapy and was fortunate to have an excellent psychiatrist. I took medication, learned better how to take care of myself, and had several beneficial close relationships, including those with my business partner (Dave Jilk) and my new girlfriend and now wife (Amy Batchelor). However, I was deeply ashamed of being depressed, of doing therapy, and for taking medication. This stigma weighed on me, some days even more than the depression.

While attending the Consumer Electronics Show in January 2013, I found myself in a dark Las Vegas hotel room, covering my head with a pillow, utterly uninterested in dealing with anything.

It was the start of a major depressive episode that lasted almost six months.

It appeared that my life was great. Foundry Group, the company I started in 2007, was doing well, and my marriage this time was solid and happy. But as I figured out later, I was physiologically and psychologically exhausted due to an utter lack of self-care, which triggered the episode. I'd been clinically depressed before and recognized the symptoms. I knew that it eventually would pass, but I didn't know when or what would bring relief.

This time I didn't feel any stigma. I'd been open about my past struggles with depression. Through my blog, I'd written a little about it and talked at many events about it. I'd worked with other entrepreneurs who had been depressed and had learned a lot about what did and didn't help. This time, I decided to be open about my depression as it was unfolding and dig deeper into the dynamics around depression.

That same January, two well-known entrepreneurs, Jody Sherman and Aaron Swartz, committed suicide. By May, my depression had lifted. After coming out of my depressive episode, I decided that one of my goals over the rest of my life would be to help eliminate the stigma surrounding mental health, especially in entrepreneurship. With friends like Jerry Colonna and Dave Morin also committed to this topic, I've addressed the stigma, and many other issues, surrounding depression and mental health.

In 2018, shortly after the suicides of Kate Spade and Anthony Bourdain, I received an email from Mahendra Ramsinghani. We had been friends for more than five years and co-authors of a book entitled *Startup Boards: Getting the Most Out of Your Board of Directors*. Mahendra told me that he was starting to work on his third book (this one), to be *The Resilient Founder*. While there were some blog posts, video interviews, and articles in major magazines around entrepreneurship and mental health, no one had yet taken on the topic in book form.

I immediately agreed to help, both get the word out and to write this Foreword whenever Mahendra was ready. A survey on my blog netted over 100 interviews for Mahendra with founders who were willing to talk about their depressive experiences. Periodically, Mahendra would reach out to me for advice around a topic or a connection to another entrepreneur who was visibly struggling with depression.

Since then conversations around depression, mental health, and suicide have escalated in a generally constructive way. More people talk openly about depression, especially among highly creative and successful people, including Olympic athletes. While the stigma around depression and other mental health issues in our society is still highly significant, the leadership from an increasing number of visible people around their struggles is starting to make a dent in that stigma.

After reading the near-final draft of this book, I sent Mahendra a quick email saying, "Your book is dynamite." When he set out to write the book, he told me his goal was to write a book that provides stories, anecdotes, triggers, advice, poetry, and support of all kinds from people who have struggled with depression. He accomplished this, and much more, as he deeply explored many aspects of a high-achieving personality, which includes entrepreneurs, and deconstructed many of the challenges that can lead to or amplify existing mental health issues.

In my most recent book, *The Entrepreneur's Weekly Nietzsche: A Book for Disruptors*, written with Dave Jilk, my first business partner mentioned earlier, one of the Nietzsche quotes we explore directly applies. In the chapter "Reflecting Your Light," we deconstruct the following Nietzsche quote.

Seeing our Light Shining – In the darkest hour of depression, sickness, and guilt, we are still glad to see others taking a light from us and making use of us as of the disk of the moon. By this roundabout route we derive some light from our own illuminating faculty.

In other words: When we are depressed, and everything seems bleak, we can take some comfort in the way other people respond to us. This piece of advice, along with hundreds of others, can be found in Mahendra's excellent book.

Mahendra – thank you for shining your light on all of us and helping entrepreneurs better understand the dynamics and eliminate the stigma around mental health.

Brad Feld
August 2021
Aspen, Colorado

Acknowledgments

Without Brad Feld's courage, transparency, vulnerability, and friendship, this book would have remained a wisp of a dream. Brad – you have been an entrepreneur, a full stack investor as an angel, a venture capitalist, a Fund of Funds manager. You have co-launched an accelerator – TechStars – that has changed the life of many founders and generated over $200 billion enterprise value – and authored multiple books. You continue to innovate, contribute, and support so many along this journey. Thank you, Brad, for bringing your expertise, wisdom, transparency, authenticity, innovation, and vigor into the start-up world – you have paved the way for a better tomorrow and give voice to the crazy ones, the misfits, the ones who stand tangent to the earth.

Jerry Colonna, the VC-turned magician and mensch. A sage, coach, guide, and friend to CEOs – sharing insights, wisdom and a much-needed gentle wake-up kick. Many a founder's rear has been propelled in the right direction by Jerry's kindness. He no longer counts exits and IPOs, IRR, or TVPI. All he counts is what matters – the names of people who sleep better at night, thanks to his nurturing and care. This Buddha from Brooklyn has saved many a startup founder from self-destruction. Deep gratitude to Jerry for his words, wisdom, and guidance in bringing this book to light. Even when he swears, it sounds like a blessing!

My deep debt of gratitude to the anonymous creative CEO who pitched in with intention and flare, and ate up all the avocados, for sharing her experiences – a brave soul. Brave in spirit. Brave in attempt. Thank you. Your light shines in this book, brightly. Thank you, Shally Madan, for taking the time and effort to sit down and share your journey and ideas that helped me frame this topic. I am sure a founder or three will benefit from your insights. To all the hundred plus founders and contributors, who so bravely opened up their hearts and souls, describing the gut-wrenching challenges of depression. A few of them include Yen Chat, Cristina Chipurici (Bucharest, Romania), Robert Diana (Media, PA), Juliette Eames, Judah Fish (Jerusalem, Israel), Felicity Noël Keeley (Washington, DC), Jake Kerr (Chicago, IL), Jake Knight (Truckee, CA), Shally Madan (CA), Tim Miller, William Morrison (Sun Valley, ID), Selina Troesch Munster (Los Angeles, CA), Christine Sommers (Vancouver, BC, Canada), and Ashley Theiss (Vancouver, BC, Canada).

My childhood buddies, Nitin Ahuja, Chirayu Chaphekar, Nitin Mohan, and Rajesh Tihari for their steadfast friendship over 25 years of so much madness, so much laughter. My gratitude to Paddy Deshmukh, Rakesh Joshi, and Ratan Dulani who have endured my craziness for much longer than most friends. Thank you to my dear cousins, Raj Hirwani and the design maestro Sid Hirwani for ideas and inspirations.

My family, Deepa and Aria, who sometimes believe that I have the ability to make raccoon-like noises. To Amar and Geeta, whose love and blessings have helped me become who I am.

The journey of writing this book has been rewarding – my life continues to grow rich with purpose, resilience, adventure, joy, abundance, kindness, trust, and more.

So thank you all, without whom this would not have been possible. As Salman Rushdie once wrote, *"I am the sum total of everything that went before me, of all I have been seen, done, of everything done-to-me. I am everyone. Everything whose being-in-the-world affected me. And was affected by mine."*

About the Cover

Self Made Man by Bobbie Carlyle

If the journey of entrepreneurship had to be captured in an image, this would be it.

This cover picture, right here, is worth more than all the 100,000 words in this book.

This process of chiseling away the granite around us.

Artist, sculptor, and creator Bobbie Carlyle says, "I was going through a particularly challenging time over 30 years ago, when I started to work on my sculpture entitled *Self Made Man*. As a battered wife who has experienced isolation, grief, counseling, families torn apart by divorce, death, and hardships, my art was also my own form of therapy. This was important for my growth and I hope it is for others as well."

As an artist, Bobbie sculpted her own path into her art business, taking a home equity line of credit, and started spending long hours working on this sculpture. First, she created a rough draft or a smaller-scale model; then, she developed the larger model. The first *Self Made Man* at scale turned out to be almost 10 feet tall. As she put finishing touches on it, Bobbie had herself crossed over from being a battered wife to the world of being a self-made entrepreneur. She could have her long-sought-after life for herself and her seven children, all the while creating art that would speak to many others of their own struggles. Her children became her models, and she would take them on her art show trips while hauling sculptures on freeways on her 18-foot-long flatbed trailer. Her son once wrote a school class essay about his hero – his mom, Bobbie. He wrote about how she had been through immense hardships, stood up for them, and made herself successful without compromising her inner voice. "When I read this, I sat and cried," says Bobbie. "I knew that I was okay and we were going to be alright."

Over the past three decades, *Self Made Man* and others of her works have been installed in universities, public installations, and homes worldwide.

"I deliberately did not make this sculpture all smooth and shiny without rough areas. Life itself has so many rough areas. We have many challenges in life. Only if we reflect on these challenges can we search and discover ourselves. They can help us to build and grow our character. We have to be determined to succeed. Women and men who have bought the *Self Made Man* often share all the hardships they have been through to get to a successful point in their lives. It's an acknowledgment of the realities of life, not just the epitome of their accomplishment. And it's not about gender either. While I have created a *Self Made Woman* as well, this process is about our own growth. My whole life has revolved around taking care of people and my art is an extension – it cares, and hopefully brings joy, solace, and strength."

One of the largest commissions of *Self Made Man* is a 14-feet-tall 1,500-pound bronze behemoth installed at the University of North Carolina, Charlotte. After the 9/11 attacks in New York, the inspiration to rebuild the spirit of America would come, in part, from this sculpture.

And so I hope that the rebuilding of your own entrepreneurial spirit comes from within, as you chisel away all that is unnecessary.

(Bobbie Caryle's works can be found at https://BobbieCarlyle Sculpture.com.)

A Note to Readers

This book is not a substitute for professional care and does not present specific medical, psychological, or emotional advice. Depression and its causes can be due to a variety of reasons, including biological or genetic, or driven by health, relationships, or economic circumstances. Each person should engage in a program of treatment, prevention, cure, or general health only in consultation with a licensed, qualified physician, therapist, or other competent professional. Neither the author nor the publisher offer this book as a diagnosis, prescription, recommendation, or cure for any specific kind of medical, psychological, or emotional problem.

Introduction
The Despondent Founder

In the mythological epic, Mahabharata, the narrative begins with its warrior-hero despondent, dejected, and frozen in the middle of a battlefield. Enemy armies surround him. He needs to act. Yet he is overwhelmed. Written in circa fourth century BC, such a timeless story about a warrior-hero, could very well be about the modern day entrepreneur.[1] One who often feels lost, confused, and despondent. Unable to apply his mind, stuck in a funk. Like a Formula One race car that sputters and coasts slowly to the side, he stalls.

Meanwhile, the commercial battle rages on. Payroll needs to be managed, cash is low, competitors are chomping at the bit, and the team needs motivation and guidance.

Why do entrepreneurs make a conscious choice to jump into the battlefield, to put themselves in positions that most would not dare to? We know that at a deep level, all entrepreneurs are fundamentally abnormal, even irrational, because rational people rarely try to change the world. The irrational spirit is aching to fill a void, both in their psyches and in society. They suffer from *cognitive dissonance*, which is a fancy term for beliefs or behavior that are inconsistent. The odds are stacked against them. Start-ups fail at a very high rate, as much as 90% or more, yet entrepreneurs choose this path. We wonder why.

Working against all possible odds and every possible challenge, the founder chooses this form of self-torture in

promise of a reward. She decides to leap over hurdles of innovation and technological development, building teams, gathering resources, selling products, ensuring growth, retaining
healthy gross margins, defending her turf against competition.
Under immense pressure to perpetually grow at a rapid pace,
start-up founders are encouraged, expected, and cheered on to
pump up revenues and valuation to keep the motivation and
the momentum. If growth drops, everything scatters. People
escape. Investors flee. Down rounds occur, and the company
is declared as damaged goods. Pressure extends over into
publicly traded companies, as the CEOs live and die by their
quarterly earnings guidance.

   While aiming for hypergrowth, the founder undergoes
a stressful journey managing the unknowns of developing
products, go-to-market tactics, managing sales momentum,
attracting high-performing teams, raising capital, fending off
acquirers, and beating the competition. If start-ups are the
new war zones, the founder is not fully prepared to wield the
weapons with courage, and finds herself pushed over the top,
burned out, exhausted, afraid – a wounded soldier. Those who
chanted the "move fast and break things" mantra find their
own psyches broken. Founders have now started to open up
and publicly describe the toll of the start-up journey.

---

*I recently chose to step down as CEO of the technology company
I co-founded . . . It wasn't an easy decision; ongoing struggles with
mental illness and a desire to prioritize my mental health were the
primary drivers of this choice.*
                                   — Matthew Cooper, co-founder, Earnup[2]

   In my research for this book, over 150 founders and
business leaders opened up to share their own journeys in these
dark domains of stress and depression. They have provided
answers, which have been encapsulated into these chapters.

   The following pages are voices of the founders who have
often struggled to understand how to seek help, while being at
odds with the demands and realities of running their businesses.

Should we soldier on silently, fighting these demonic battles alone? How should we seek therapy in the chest-thumping, macho, passion-driven start-up world? How should we respond to the classical loaded question–answer greeting "So, how is it going? Crushing it, aren't you?"

Should we "always be crushing it" and then one day our selves feel crushed? Simone Weil, the French philosopher, urged that the only suitable question to ask another human being was, "What are you going through?"

PSYCHOLOGICAL QUOTIENT – AN INTRODUCTION

This book is a rough guide to developing awareness of your inner resources; you could call it your psychological quotient. Just as we have developed frameworks for IQ and EQ, knowing a bit about our own psychology can help develop emotional resilience. Even possibly address the unspoken challenges of depression in any business leader's journey. Most entrepreneurs often struggle with the dark nights and suffer from anxiety, depression, and breakdown. Some get help; they keep going. Some train themselves to get out of the funk. Some give up. Like any grueling marathon, the number of people at the finish line is far smaller than those at the start.

Starting a company is like eating glass and staring into the abyss.
— *Elon Musk*

We know IQ and we know EQ – the impact of our intellect and emotions in the world of business is well understood. Psychological quotient can be best defined as the ability to identify and develop our inner resources – the ability of entrepreneurs to tackle challenges and flourish. With psychology and the study of our behaviors, we can identify and eliminate subconsciously self-constructed barriers and skillfully navigate the game of business. And if our resources fall short, how should we identify early warning signs of our flailing mental states?

Is this burnout? Is this depression? Where is my "battery about to die" sign? What are some tools and techniques to build self-awareness of our psychology and build endurance? When the waves of external stress factors engulf the founders, we find we can no longer swim as skillfully as we once did. "It never stops," says one founder. The competition is trying to kill you, your team members are arguing, asking for raises and everyone wants to be on a CEO career path," says one founder. Although we cannot control the external factors, how we perceive and react to them is the heart of this game.

In the following pages, we will explore lessons of endurance shared by over 150 founders – how they wrestled with the dark angels, one day at a time, and reached the other side. We live in a world where passion is an overblown fetish. Bravado and chutzpah is the only currency of champions. Emotions are buried deep. To express the full range of our emotions would be considered unprofessional, weak, immature.

Amidst these social constraints, these founders share their authentic and honest insights. Theirs is the real bravado. In sharing their journey, they offer strength, solace, and guidance. While founders who absorb these lessons may benefit, I believe it can also provide some guidance to the investor community. For venture capitalists, the ones who have gladly provided the ammunition for the disruption wars, encountering the wounded soldier is somewhat uncharted territory. We thought we were being helpful, strategizing, connecting, adding value, cheering, supporting, but how did we get here? What stance should an investor take when founders reach the end of the rope? Instead of pointing the founders to the nearest friendly therapist, or funding the next meditation app, how can investors take a proactive approach to address the crux of the problem?

In putting this book together, my somewhat meager attempt to highlight the importance of psychological quotient might have fallen short. This is a vast, complex issue. And we have no simple straight answers. Bear with me as we unpack this heavy stuff.

No One Is Normal

How does the structure of human thought and behavior develop, especially with entrepreneurs? Can a founder afford the luxury of a normal ego? (No, not in my view.) How does the social and cultural view impact the founders and the CEOs? Silicon Valley is much different from what happens in Boulder, Berlin, Beijing, or Bengaluru.

As one CEO told me, when we get up in the morning, everyone looks out of the window and we see the same sky. But my horizon is different from yours. My inner drive and your inner drive are not the same. Why do some founders react differently while others give up?

> Whoever fights monsters should see to it that in the process he does not become a monster.
>
> And if you gaze long enough into an abyss, the abyss will gaze back into you.
>
> — Friedrich Nietzsche

What Cannot Be Measured

In the world of business, emotions are unwelcome appendages, to be checked in at the entryways of the boardrooms. Spreadsheets matter. The soul does not. Assets and annual recurring revenues (ARR) matter; anguish does not. As our balance sheets become stronger, our spirit becomes weak. And all the cash in the bank cannot buy any contentment. As human beings we are equal parts intellect and emotion, strategy and sorrow, joy and pain, achievements and unfulfilled aspirations. When we ignore the mysterious side and only measure the logical and tangible, we fail to serve our deeper self, relegating our start-ups into soulless machines. Yet the future depends on the state of our consciousness here and now. As Eckhart Tolle reminds us, "If the means did not contribute to human happiness, neither will the end. The outcome is inseparable from the actions that led to it and is already contaminated by those actions."

Doing, Thinking, and Feeling

Entrepreneur, investor, and author Brad Feld, with his authenticity and boldness gave me the impetus and permission to explore this topic. Brad has been one of the first venture capitalists to open up about his mental health, thereby giving the rest of us permission to feel. The world has encouraged us to think, become deep-thinkers and show off our rational sides, even compete on the logical plane. Yet here was a man who could bring deep feelings and show us his human side. When Brad and I co-authored *Start-up Boards*, the seeds for this book were planted. Founders shared their boardroom challenges, and when we started to dig deeper into the founder's own well-being, it was apparent that depression was rampant, unstated yet obvious – the huge elephant in the room.

In a business culture that values doing (execution) and thinking (strategy), we need to evolve toward feeling – a part that remains ignored in the world of business. By operating with our heads alone, we cast aside the best part of ourselves – the golden heart. And deep feeling leads us to awareness of feelings, unstated desires, hidden motivations, and frustrations, and the best part – our dark side. To know and have a healthy relationship with the darker parts can be a rewarding step toward our own self-development. But we don't quite know where to begin. We buried these feelings and it was best not to express these, not to talk about it. Jerry Colonna (who authored the foreword to *Start-up Boards*) has recently published *Reboot: Leadership and the Art of Growing Up*, a must-have guide for CEOs. Jerry, a former venture capitalist, is now a CEO-mensch, helping the leaders address a wide range of emotional challenges as they build their companies. One of his first observations when I started to write this book was, "When it comes to depression, our language is insufficient. Our words are inadequate. As a society, we have no practices in place to discuss, support, and nurture. How do we make it safe to step into this void and talk about it? "

Just Give Me the Answers, or Leave Me with the Unspoken Agony

Writings, podcasts, and books do not always have readily packaged solutions. But they do serve a purpose. In the book *Zorba the Greek*, Nikos Kazantzakis writes about a fictional philosopher, Zorba, who goes into a fit of rage, challenges a scholar, demanding "What is the use of all your damn books if they don't give me answers, what do they do?" To which the scholar replies, "They tell me about the agony of men who can't answer questions."

And so this book speaks to the unspoken agony. Entrepreneurs, shrinks, or shamans cannot answer the question of what precisely leads to depression. Yet when the entrepreneur suffers, innovation suffers. Progress in society suffers. Capital has no place to park itself, for its growth is tied to the growth of these crazy ones. We cheer on and love it when the founders go to war, emerge victorious. But when they fail, we simply look the other way. We do not have ways to care and nurture for the wounded warriors. We move on. Sorry but we don't quite know what to do with you, we might say. By casting them aside when they break, we do a great disservice to those who attempted to serve us. Yes, we should care for progress, but we should also care for the harbingers of its progress, in sickness and in health.

MY HOPE FOR YOU

Here, in this book, you will hear the voices of the entrepreneurs and founders who struggle and persevere. Psychology, depression, and therapy are messy, complex topics. I am no expert on these. In researching and writing about these, I did my best to keep the reader's interest front and center at all times. Some insights we have gathered from entrepreneurs may seem simplistic – motherhood and apple pie. Eat healthy food. Cut down on coffee. Get enough sleep. Critics might be tempted to dismiss these as obvious, but ask those consumed by the start-up frenzy.

Our passion can devour us. Each day, we gradually chip away at our own bodies and psyches. And then all of a sudden, we are in a full-blown crisis.

Besides the basics, we have covered some additional topics that offer insights into how we might operate. If you find that some topics are not as in-depth as it might be, please know that I am painfully aware of this deficiency. I am sure each chapter could have been its own book of sorts. Striking a balance between depth and breadth is always an issue for writers. Most certainly, this book is neither a quick-fix five-step guide to nirvana, nor has it any instant answers. Unlike a bathrobe, there is no one-size-fits-all approach to our mental health challenges. As much as we want the world to fall in neat, four-quadrant boxes, it does not.

Writing about this topic caused me enough angst and anxiety, paralyzing at times. As T. S. Eliot once wrote, "Words strain, crack and sometimes break under the burden." I stalled several times, and the pandemic did not help either. The gentle nudging, kindness, and love of a few soulmates kept me going – that, combined with the strength of the purpose. As I plodded through this journey and often wandered or got lost, all I had to do was to listen and respond to all that is around me – to a suicide; and one more suicide; to the unstated anger; the sighs; the sobs; the quivering hands, fluttery eyes, and jittery body language; to the soft pain that permeated the fundraising pitches and the impatient board rooms. Above all, the cry of those souls in silent anguish.

My sincere prayer is that entrepreneurs can use this book to build their awareness about their own psychological capital, develop resilience, and strengthen their internal resources with the tools and guideposts. Or as Emily Dickinson once wrote:

If I can ease one life the aching, Or cool one pain . . .

then this book would not be in vain.

Part I

Running to a Standstill

In which we look at how inner challenges and frustrations can push us to the limit – and how we can postpone some ideas.

1

When Suicide Seems Like a Good Option

A few years ago, a founder, who I'll call Mark, committed suicide. Mark had given up, was done, could not solve for anything anymore. His inner resources exhausted and spent, the range of problems he perceived were all massive, impossible. For Mark, the best option, in fact the only option was to end it all.

Mark was building a company that could have changed the way we design and develop medicine. To say that he was driven and passionate would be an understatement. He had raised money from some of the leading investors in Silicon Valley. As an investor in the company's seed round, I saw his fierce intensity up close.

Working 24/7, his entire life was entwined in his start-up, the milestone, the next financing round, the next step function of value creation. His identity and that of the company were fused as one. The company's success was Mark's success. The mantra of his start-up life was *quemar los barcos – burn those goddam boats.* No going back. All in. No plan B, no safety net. Those are for the weaklings. All of this was music to the investors' ears. Money flowed quickly. Mark had courage, conviction, energy, enthusiasm, and technical acumen – all the founder attributes revered in the business and technical circles. When he stood up to present his ideas, audience members would nod in agreement of a brave new world — reverently, silently. In hushed tones, they would exchange delighted notes that Mark was on to something big, groundbreaking. By any standards, here was a guy, *TheGuy*, who was well on his way to make a dent in the world.

And then one day, Mark was gone. The candle snuffed out, just like that.

We just saw one side, the bold and brazen exterior, the showman, while on the inside, the picture was vastly different. He was broken. Tired. Some evenings, when he would go visit his parents, he would just sit on the couch, for long periods of time, silently staring into the void. Overworked and exhausted, he would ask to just be left alone. He did not want to talk to anyone, nor go for a walk, watch a show, or read a book. He just wanted to decompress. The Silicon Valley cheerleaders had egged him on with generous superlatives like *man, you're crushing it*. But the chasm between his self-view, his abilities, and the scale of problems kept widening. He got crushed instead.

BREAKING THE TABOO: DISCUSSING SUICIDE

To start a book with a founder's suicide is no way to start a book. It's dark, gloomy and only exacerbates the downward spiral. Yet the conventional norms of burying the difficult emotions, pretending such challenges do not exist, need to be dismantled. In bringing the challenge to the forefront, we can allow the discomfort to rise. And then settle down. We can allow the emotion to surge, even for a few moments. And we can begin to talk about the topics we should no longer be hiding from, because when we open ourselves up, we give each one another permission to bring forth the uncomfortable turmoil. And when we allow these frustrations to vent away, it might help, heal, or even save a life.

A start-up is a grand experiment, a gamble of a different kind, with our time on earth and other people's money, in markets that have yet to be formed, with products that do not exist. We do this without fully understanding ourselves, and what is for us or what is against us. And more often, we end up on a dead-end street, frustrated and crushed. Suicide is a taboo, a pariah of a subject, but a reality. On the surface of it all, we treat this subject with heavy doses of platitudes, quotable quotes, quick-fix solutions, or conclusive statistics. To confess any remote suicidal thoughts causes immense discomfort, more often to the listener. When we do not listen to the pain, the force that could have changed the world gets forced out of this world. We are humans first, and then we label ourselves as founders, employees, and everything else.

Brandon Fluharty · 2nd   + Follow
VP @ LivePerson | Founder @ Be
Focused. Live Great.
1w · Edited · 🌐

I've tried committing suicide twice.

I've had a panic attack in front of a big client.

I suffered a mini stroke when I was 32.

I say all of this because they are still a part of who I am as a person.

Not something from my past that needs to be shoved into a box and locked away.

We're humans first.

Professionals second.

And because of that, we must take mental health seriously as individuals and employers.

Things that will help:

- Make getting help very easy for everyone
- Create an environment where it feels safe to talk about tough stuff
- Understand that leading with empathy is good for business
- Prioritize yourself in order to deliver more to others

Remember:

When we're better humans, we're better professionals...

From Linkedin: A step towards being better humans first....

When Dreams Turn to Despair

How does it happen?

- Desires and ambitions propel us into actions (start a company).
- Actions without results lead to restlessness (slow pace of adoption, maybe).
- Prolonged restlessness leads to dejections and disillusionments (this will never work).
- All these culminate in despair (no one cares).
- And then the final question: Is this worth it?

The mind that could surge up in confidence to start a company, that could discriminate the merits of an opportunity, build a compelling narrative, raise capital from some of the world's best investors in Silicon Valley – that same mind had lost its ability to find a way out of this chaos.

Why does the powerful force that could have made a dent in the world turn inward and self-destruct?

- Varying degrees of adversity – from product market fit, to raising capital, to scaling, and dealing with competition
- A conflict in relationships – co-founders, board, team or family members
- Threats to perceived notions of success
- Financial or legal challenges
- The daily roller coaster ride of wild swings that are not experienced in most careers

Aleksandr Volodarsky
@volodarik

Running a startup feels like the biggest mental disorder:

9am: *competitor funding news* I can't believe we are so slow

9:10: *new lead* screw VC, we'll grow 4x without them

9:12: *churn report* we won't make it

9:18: *new lead* we'll all be billionaires

Source: Twitter, Inc.

These obstacles impact almost all of us at some point in our lives. And we often feel like it's the end. In his post "What's the Most Difficult CEO Skill?," entrepreneur-turned-venture capitalist Ben Horowitz writes that managing your own psychology is the most difficult skill. CEOs often succumb to that WFIO. Pronounced as *whee-f-eyo*, it's that sinking feeling. We are f**ked ... It's Over! And in such situations, one option that surfaces is to self-destruct.

Sigmund Freud wrote that "the tendency to self-destruction exists to a certain degree in many more persons than in those who bring it to completion."

In the United States, the ratios of suicide attempts to suicide deaths are approximately 100:1.[1]

A lot of us think about it. A few actually do it. It is okay that we have an occasional thought.[2] We are just afraid to talk about it.

Thinking, Ruminating, Full-on Planning

When we are in a funk, we keep thinking about suicide. Those thoughts might keep spinning in our heads, and soon some of us even start to research the how-to options. We might identify the various steps, and plan the final exit in great detail.

Tim Ferriss, investor, podcaster, and author of the best-selling book *The 4-Hour Workweek*, writes about how he had gotten past the "deciding mode" and into "full-on planning mode." "The world was better off without a loser," he had concluded.

In his planning mode, Tim Ferriss went to Princeton's Firestone Library. As one of the promising titles on this dark topic of suicide was checked out, Tim put a reserve request for the book. Back in those days, well before the Web, Kindle, and email, the only way to reserve a book was to put your name on a paper log. Once the book was available, the library would then mail you a postcard. *Come get this book you were waiting for. We will hold it for two weeks.* The postcard, with the promising title of suicide, landed in his mom's hands. Sure, Mom might be wondering about this fantastical development in her son's reading habits.

"Oo – and thank f**king God," writes Tim. His worried mom called Tim to ask about this book and he blurted out a fast lie – a friend wanted this book for research on depression. Tim had specced out as many as six exit pathways, but that one call from his mom flipped a switch in his head. "I snapped out of my delusion by this one-in-a-million accident," he writes. A library's postcard may have saved Tim's life.

Entrepreneur Ben Huh writes of his days of despondency. "I spent a week in my room with the lights off and cut off from the world, thinking of the best way to exit this failure. Death was a good option – and it got better by the day."

Brilliant blazing minds on fire, when faced with severe obstacles and resistance, often get frustrated and impatient. Any goal seems insurmountable. The road seems exhausting, long. Check out what some founders have said.

Founders' Voices

- As we were going to bed, my spouse – a founder – muttered, "Sometimes I think it would be a lot easier if I didn't wake up tomorrow morning ..."
- The idea of suicide changed from a comforting option to a constant yet terrifying urge ...
- My head was filled with thoughts of suicide – that I was thinking about it in some form or another all the time shook me up ... felt like a vice clamped around my head.

To the young who want to die

-Gwendolyn Brooks

Sit down. Inhale. Exhale.
The gun will wait. The lake will wait.
The tall gall in the small seductive vial
will wait will wait:
will wait a week: will wait through April.
You do not have to die this certain day.
Death will abide, will pamper your postponement.
I assure you death will wait. Death has
a lot of time. Death can
attend to you tomorrow. Or next week. Death is just
down the street; is most obliging neighbor; can meet
you any moment.
You need not die today.
Stay here – through pout or pain or peskyness.
Stay here. See what the news is going to be tomorrow.
Graves grow no green that you can use. Remember,
green's your color. You are Spring.

What Drives Us to the Cliff – Is It Shame, Envy, or Powerlessness?

We never would fully know the range of emotions that drives founders to the cliff. One can speculate, a bit too simplistically, that a faltering self-image is one factor – that we no longer see ourselves as brave, bold, and skilled. We are disillusioned with our inabilities, expectations, and the world's incessant demands. We pull over to the side of the road. The state of helplessness spirals, often oscillating between disappointment and anger. We become harsh on our own selves. Suicide becomes a form of protest, revenge, and/or appeal.

In a rapid-paced world, the fastest runner, the unicorn-bagging CEO, becomes the hero. But very few get there, and for the vast majority who don't, the self-image crumbles. "This state of shame and envy is followed by self-destructive impulses … the suffering ego wants to do away with the self in order to wipe out the offending, disappointing reality of failure … the self-destructive impulses are to be understood here as the expression of narcissistic rage," writes psycho-analyst Heinz Kohut. Founders have to be mildly narcissistic, and believe that their images, their views can change the world. When faced with resistance, this perspective and energy turns dark, angry, a rage when it does not meet its self-appointed goals.

Those who may have started off on the hero's journey may soon feel powerless against the stagnant forces of the market adoption risks, technology stasis, and fickleness of investors, who were chasing the next big thing. Mark probably felt weak and helpless. And his identity was so attached to his start-up, unable to separate the two, he decided to end it all.

Vulnerable Egos and High Expectations

Founders hold themselves to high expectations – statements like *make a dent in the world* are a part of their daily dialogue. The chasm between their expectations and outcomes may be wide, and the resources required to build the bridge or cross this chasm may not be available, but that does not scare nor stop them.

To propel the founder to greater heights, a self-image of a hero is an essential mind hack. As one VC told me, every founder aspiring to change the world should first *believe* that they can do it; that they have the courage, the magical powers to pick the right direction, to influence others, to gather resources and deploy these effectively; to persist and stay the course. We are often unaware how we subconsciously build and shape our belief systems. In building our belief systems, a healthy self-image is an asset. It helps us pick aspirational goals, but our ability to manage our own psychological barriers becomes a hurdle. Inflated self-images combined with vulnerable egos can make us our own worst enemies. We tend to be overly favorable in our self-view in many domains, as the Dunning-Kruger effect shows us.

SELF-IMAGE AND INEPTITUDE

McArthur Wheeler robbed two banks in Pittsburgh in broad daylight. He had worn neither a mask nor any form of disguise and was promptly arrested in a few hours. It was not just incompetence but lack of application of knowledge of lemon juice. Wheeler was under the flawed impression that applying lemon juice to his face made him invisible to the video surveillance cameras. Thanks to this inspiration and case of stupidity, researchers David Dunning and Justin Kruger went on to publish a fascinating study, "Unskilled and Unaware of It: How Difficulties in Recognizing One's Own Incompetence Lead to Inflated Self-Assessments."[3]

The summary of the study is quite simple. We think we are way smarter than we actually are. And because of such inflated self-images we tend to make stupid choices. Like rubbing lemon juice on one's face and then robbing a bank. And our stupidity makes it nearly impossible for us to realize that we are – pause for a drumroll – stupid. Dunning and Kruger state this in a far more polished manner. Read on.

> *People tend to hold overly favorable views of their abilities in many social and intellectual domains. Not only do these people reach erroneous conclusions and make unfortunate choices, but [also] their incompetence robs them of the metacognitive ability to realize it.*

Across four different studies, the authors found that participants scoring in the bottom quartile on tests grossly overestimated their test performance and ability. Although their test scores put them in the 12th percentile, they estimated themselves to be in the 62nd (see the following figure). In other words, we assume ourselves to be fives times better than we actually are. Imagine trying to fly an airplane with such an inflated self-image. Or performing brain surgery. The BBC summarized the findings of the Dunning-Kruger study with the headline "The More Inept You Are the Smarter You Think You Are."

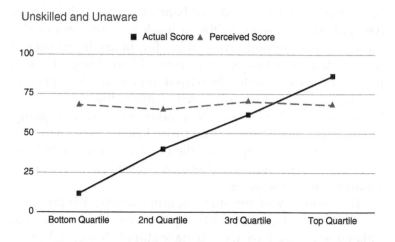

But here is the best part. The researchers conclude that improving the skills of participants increased their metacognitive competence, and helped them recognize the limitations of their abilities. In other words, as our skills improve, we come to realize our own stupidity. As W. B. Yeats writes in his 1920 poem "The Second Coming,"

> *The best lack all conviction, while the worst*
> *Are full of passionate intensity.*

To invert this effect, and calibrate your self-image, try to think about any skill in which you believe you are the best. Adjust that self-score downward by 5X and then start working toward building your skill. As your skill improves – voilà – the self-image gets calibrated magically.

Researchers have found that those who have high expectations of themselves and have a vulnerable ego are susceptible to suicide. What is this ego? And should it be vulnerable? Can it become stronger? Being unaware of such basic psychological notions, we are unable to decipher, let alone harness this strange inner force. Pick any book with its esoteric pearls of wisdom and you will find references to *destroy your ego*. *The ego is an enemy*. This is a fundamentally flawed notion in the context of entrepreneurship. Just as money is not the root of evil, but an excessive lust for money is, the ego is not the enemy. An inflated out-of-control ego, like an unbridled horse, is the enemy. A weak ego, unable to handle responsibilities and frustrations, overwhelmed perpetually is the enemy. **The healthy ego, in fact, can be a founder's greatest ally, an essential resource in changing the world.** A healthy ego is your wingman, your charioteer, your guide. It helps the entrepreneur to navigate the journey. It tackles everything with the ease and grace of an agile problem solver. A healthy ego could even become a force for good in society.

Having strong views of their own selves is supremely important for founders. It is indeed a precondition. A vulnerable ego can turn that same strength against its own self, destroying the inner drive. Freud holds the view that when we do not get what we yearn for, we turn against that very object of yearning. Sometimes that object can be our own life.

When Tim Ferris was contemplating suicide, he could well be yearning for something that he could not get. The self-view as a loser soon starts to propagate. The loser's mind then starts to descend into a steady drumbeat: "The world does not need another loser."

From the trio of image, expectations, and ego, founders can turn some knobs around. We can paint our own self-image as work in perpetual progress. We can forgive ourselves and others and accept that we are not fully formed Greek Gods. At least not yet.

Our expectations of our work can be tied to self-transcendence as opposed to being stuck on hedonistic treadmills.

Our self-confidence need not collapse into self-doubt, leading into a downward spiral of fear and anxiety.

Above all, I often wonder if our ego can save us from frustrations, exhaustion, and this gnawing sense of hopelessness.

If yes, how do we go to this "ego-gym" and build this strange muscle inside us, in a healthy way?

Especially when the world out there has declared the ego to be the enemy.

The Tyranny of Ambition, the Agony of Success

The siren call of suicide is not exclusively restricted to those who have suffered setbacks or failure. Successful founders have often struggled with a sense of loss after the victory lap has been completed. An investor I knew really well committed suicide. He was a great friend, someone I would call as often as three times a week. We talked often, bantered, had fun, and had co-invested in dozens of companies. We spent time together on the cap-table as well as the dinner table. When in town, he would often stay with me. He was a part of *mia familia* yet I was clueless about his mental anguish. To this day, I wonder why he committed suicide, when he had made his millions.

In his self-view, he may have lost his motivation, facing some inner hurdles. In his worldview, maybe there was no further joy, contentment, or challenges. Successful founders often experience a feeling of emptiness, a void.

L'appel du vide

This French phrase roughly translates to "the call of the void" – that strange fleeting urge to jump when standing atop high buildings, peaks. When you get up to the higher levels of the Eiffel Tower, some might get the call of the void. They have nets all over to prevent people from jumping, and for most, this fleeting urge passes in seconds.

Such a call of the void often comes after those millions have been banked. The lack of an ongoing challenge, no monsters to wrestle with, puts an energetic founder in a state of helpless despair. There are no problems to solve anymore, what should I do with myself? Maybe create a new start-up? And thus we stay trapped on the treadmill.

Irvin Yalom, author and therapist in Silicon Valley, writes that "the success of young high-tech millionaires generates a life crisis that can be instructive about non-self-transcendent life-meaning systems." In other words, the millionaires are stuck with "What next?" Making the millions did not transcend their own selves. They start new companies, try to repeat their success. Why? They tell themselves they must prove it was no fluke, that they can do it alone, without a particular investor, partner, or mentor. They raise the bar. They no longer need 1 or 2 million in the bank – they need 5, 10, even 50 million to feel secure. They realize the pointlessness and irrationality in earning more money when they already have more than they can possibly spend, but this does not stop them. They realize they are taking away time from their families, from things closer to the heart, but they just cannot give up playing the game. "The money is just lying out there," they tell themselves. "All I have to do is pick it up."

A successful entrepreneur who made a ton of money or a failed one who did not make any both ended up at the same juncture.

Money, fame, and success are not necessarily an antidote for our inner chaos.

DOES OUR ATTITUDE DEFINE OUR OUTCOMES?

When things are working out well, our self-confidence starts to soar. We end up tasting the elusive yet delicious elixir of success – fame, fortune, and glory. Our sense of well-being flourishes. We become benevolent members of society, sharing our gifts, glowing in the attention. We feel good about ourselves and our achievements and perch atop the apex of the self-actualization pyramid, our joy flowing, serving the society for a greater good. Even if all this is for a fleeting moment, we sure aspire for, and relish this moment.

But more often things don't quite work out. Our ambitions are often greater. Reality bites. And if our plans do not come to fruition, we succumb to an angry, arrogant, disillusioned state. Our self-confidence shrivels up, and we can descend into fear, despair and depression.

From such a dark state, we can decide to move into a state of self-reflection and improvement, and develop a path toward adjusting our self-images and skills. See Figure 1.1.

But more often than not, it is easy to stay stuck in that lower left corner. Is there a way to move to another box, ideally the one in the top right corner? Entrepreneur Ben Huh, whose suicidal tendencies trapped him in a dark room for a whole week, finally walked out. He does not recall why he left the room, but wrote that the most meaningful act he performed was to *leave that room*. In doing so, he saw the positive in the very act of moving out of darkness. "Dealing with reality was the best antidote to a make-believe world. Instead of fantasizing about death, I decided to deal with the harshness of reality," he writes.

Figure 1-1 **Do our attitudes define our outcomes?**

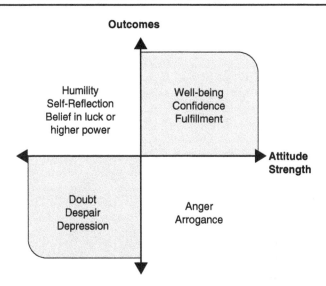

Ben blogged openly about his inner struggles. His expressions resonated with founders worldwide.

The first thing he changed was his behavior.

He left the room.

Maybe getting up and leaving the darkness, making the choice to deal with reality, is the first step toward recovery.

Developing the right attitude, strengthening it - it all takes time. We would not be here if we had those traits. But let us take the first step - like Ben, let us leave the dark room. And move one step closer to well-being.

Fig 3.1 Do our attitudes define our outcomes?

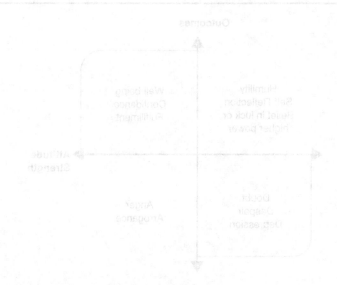

Rei blogged openly about his inner struggles. His expressions resonated with readers worldwide.

The first thing he changed was his behavior.

He left the room.

Maybe getting up and leaving the darkness, making the choice to seek help today, is the first step toward recovery.

Developing the right attitude, strengthening it—it all takes time. We won't not be here if we had those tools. But let us take the first step—like Rei, let us leave the dark room. And move one step closer to well-being.

2

Stepping Back from the Edge

Mark, the founder who had set out to change this world, had committed suicide. As an investor in his company, I was still grieving, trying to process this, going for long solo walks and having conversations with Mark's spirit. Part of me was sad. Part of me was guilty. Part of me was angry. And it did not make it any easier when another investor sent out an lawyer like email, demanding a special shareholder meeting, seeking an inspection of the books and the status of the cash. Investors, fiduciaries, and all that jazz – yup, we have duties and responsibilities. To the company. But what about our duties to the spirit and the soul? When I sat down with Mark's family member, I fumbled for words. I did not know what to say, where to begin. They did not know me. And probably wondered why I had shown up; I, who was a part of the problem. *Are you here to represent those cold-hearted shareholders?*, they may have wondered. Where was I when Mark was struggling? Had I failed in my role as a human being, one who could not bond with another?

Later that night, I read Meggie Royer's poem, "The Morning After I Killed Myself," in which she narrates the regrets of a suicide and how she tries to *unkill* herself. She writes about the orange tree and the red cloud – the sun rising, setting. She writes about eggs and toast and cheese. About love for her mother. I wished that Mark had read this poem too. Because if he had read it, maybe, just maybe, he might have changed his mind.

The Morning After I Killed Myself, I Woke Up

-by Meggie Royer

The morning after I killed myself, I woke up. I made myself breakfast in bed. I added salt and pepper to my eggs and used my toast for a cheese and bacon sandwich. I squeezed a grapefruit into a juice glass. I scraped the ashes from the frying pan and rinsed the butter off the counter. I washed the dishes and folded the towels.

The morning after I killed myself, I fell in love. Not with the boy down the street or the middle school principal. Not with the everyday jogger or the grocer who always left the avocados out of the bag. I fell in love with my mother and the way she sat on the floor of my room holding each rock from my collection in her palms until they grew dark with sweat. I fell in love with my father down at the river as he placed my note into a bottle and sent it into the current. With my brother who once believed in unicorns but who now sat in his desk at school trying desperately to believe I still existed.

The morning after I killed myself, I walked the dog. I watched the way her tail twitched when a bird flew by or how her pace quickened at the sight of a cat. I saw the empty space in her eyes when she reached a stick and turned around to greet me so we could play catch but saw nothing but sky in my place. I stood by as strangers stroked her muzzle and she wilted beneath their touch like she did once for mine.

The morning after I killed myself, I went back to the neighbors' yard where I left my footprints in concrete as a two year old and examined how they were already fading. I picked a few daylilies and pulled a few weeds and watched the elderly woman through her window as she read the paper with the news of my death. I saw her husband spit tobacco into the kitchen sink and bring her her daily medication.

The morning after I killed myself, I watched the sun come up. Each orange tree opened like a hand and the kid down the street pointed out a single red cloud to his mother.

The morning after I killed myself, I went back to that body in the morgue and tried to talk some sense into her. I told her about the avocados and the stepping stones, the river and her parents. I told her about the sunsets and the dog and the beach.

The morning after I killed myself, I tried to unkill myself, but couldn't finish what I started.

LOOKING FOR CLARITY

The last thing a suicidal person wants is to be reminded that their final act will cause more damage. Caught between the jaws of their own unmanageable pain, hopelessness, and fear, writes author Al Alvarez in his book *The Savage God – A Study of Suicide*,

> *Suicide is, after all, the result of a choice. However impulsive the action and confused the motives, at the moment when a man finally decides to take his own life he achieves a certain temporary clarity. Suicide may be a declaration of bankruptcy which passes judgment on a life as one long history of failure. But it is a decision which, by its very finality, is not wholly a failure. There is, I believe, a whole class of suicides who take their own lives not in order to die but to escape confusion, to clear their heads. They deliberately use suicide to create an unencumbered reality for themselves or to break through the patterns of obsession and necessity which they have unwittingly imposed on their lives.*

Part of me feels like there is nothing we could have done to prevent a suicide. This was destined to happen. Part of me screams that hell yes, we could have reached out to him. Sometimes, it's just one conversation. With a poet, a philosopher, or a friend.

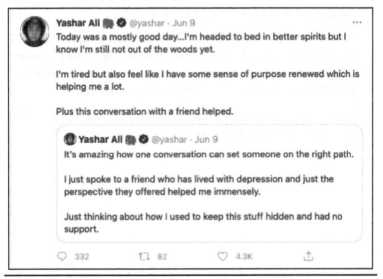

Yashar Ali @ @yashar · Jun 9

Today was a mostly good day...I'm headed to bed in better spirits but I know I'm still not out of the woods yet.

I'm tired but also feel like I have some sense of purpose renewed which is helping me a lot.

Plus this conversation with a friend helped.

Yashar Ali @ @yashar · Jun 9

It's amazing how one conversation can set someone on the right path.

I just spoke to a friend who has lived with depression and just the perspective they offered helped me immensely.

Just thinking about how I used to keep this stuff hidden and had no support.

332   82   4.3K

Source: Twitter, Inc.

This Might Be Just a Passing Phase, One of My Bad Days

Most depression episodes last for less than 10 months (see Figure 2.1). For those who have been dragged down to the depths of depression, each day is a drudgery, and 10 months may seem like eternity. But when we put things in context of our entire life, 10 months is a short phase. A tough phase, for sure. But it doesn't spell the end of it all.

Figure 2-1 **Most depression episodes drop after ~10 months.**[1]

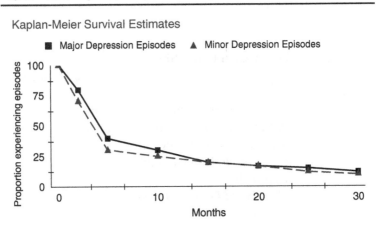

Kaplan-Meier Survival Estimates

I Go Down to the Shore

-by Mary Oliver

I go down to the shore in the morning
and depending on the hour the waves
are rolling in or moving out,
and I say, oh, I am miserable,
what shall -
what should I do? And the sea says
in its lovely voice:
Excuse me, I have work to do

Fantasizing about Death versus Facing the Harshness of Reality

Then there is always this possibility that suicide might not work out. That embarrassment of a failed attempt and the dark humor that comes with it . . . guess I failed at suicide too?

The list of all those who failed at suicide is long. Tim Ferriss and Jerry Colonna failed at suicide. They went on and succeeded in many other ways. For one, they lived to talk about their journey and inspire the rest of us.

If suicide is a form of repressed frustration, openness about suicidal thoughts might be a welcome form, a release of sorts. Easier said than done, but after all, we are merely talking about what most of us may have felt at some point or another in life. Just like any other frustration compounded by a mix of emotions. Like love, joy, or sadness. By speaking about our repressed frustrations, we take a step toward relief. We bring it out from within, we stare at it, understand it. How do these frustrations seize our power of judgment, numb us so completely and crush our motivation? When we fail to make peace with reality, and keep ruminating in hopelessness, we get into a downward spiral and an all-consuming negative vortex. Our aspirations fuel us on, but the range of unintended outcomes becomes hard to handle (see Table 2.1).

Table 2-1 **Aspirations and Outcomes**

Aspirations	Unintended outcomes
Financial freedom	Overwhelmed/overstimulated
Problem-solving skills	Feeling adrift
Logical processes	Disorganized chaos
Self-confidence	Fear, anxiety, and defensive behaviors
Adaptability/agility	Rigidity/fear of change/aggression
New learnings and growth	Stagnancy and pessimism
Enhanced empathy for team members and customers	Inability to understand and express emotions; self-centered/one-sided

When in such a vortex, the best thing to do is to postpone any plans till tomorrow. And between now and tomorrow, those aching parts inside you – how can you help those gnawing, angry, frustrated parts to be still? Talking about suicide is as easy as chewing glass, but starting with "I am not feeling as good today" may just as well be a starting point.

Dr. Irvin D. Yalom, MD, professor emeritus of psychiatry at Stanford University, often tells his suicidal patients, "There is a part of you that is here today. I want to talk to that part of you ..."

You are here today.

And so am I.

And while we are still here, we have to contribute our verse.

O Me! O Life!

-Walt Whitman

Oh me! Oh life! of the questions of these recurring,
Of the endless trains of the faithless, of cities fill'd with the foolish,
Of myself forever reproaching myself,
(for who more foolish than I, and who more faithless?)
Of eyes that vainly crave the light,
of the objects mean,
of the struggle ever renew'd,
Of the poor results of all,
of the plodding and sordid crowds I see around me,
Of the empty and useless years of the rest,
with the rest me intertwined,
The question, O me! so sad, recurring—What good amid these,
O me, O life?

Answer

That you are here – that life exists and identity,
That the powerful play goes on, and you may contribute a verse.

What verse will you contribute?

3

How External Events Trigger Negative Feelings

What brings misery to a founder? Competition? Lack of financing? Market acceptance of product? Or the inability to do a hundred small things required each day?

Stressful life events have a substantial relationship with the onset of episodes of major depression, researchers proclaim, as seen in Table 3.1. A start-up life includes a generous dose of depressive triggers; loss of job occurs by design or default. There is neither a financial cushion nor a predictable drip of a salary each month. All founders have faced financial problems, be it personal or be it payroll. Or legal hassles. Marital challenges are not too far behind.

But here is the counterintuitive part: about one-third of the association between stressful life events and onsets of depression is noncausal, since **"individuals predisposed to major depression select themselves into high-risk environments."**[1] Put differently, we throw ourselves into high-risk environments to feed our innate tendencies. Is it the start-up life that leads us to a depressive episode, or is it our predisposition that puts us in such a situation?

Table 3-1 **External Events and Depression Triggers**

Life Events	Odds that such events trigger depression	
	Month of event	Three months after the event
Job loss	3.95	N/A
Legal problems	3.81	10.81
Work problems	2.44	2.74
Financial problems	5.85	2.36
Divorce	5.22	N/A
Marital problems	8.39	4.29
Assault	25.36	N/A

(*Source:* K. S. Kendler, J. Kuhn, and C. A. Prescott, "The Interrelationship of Neuroticism, Sex, and Stressful Life Events in the Prediction of Episodes of Major Depression," *American Journal of Psychiatry* 161, no. 4 (2004): 631–636.)

PERSISTENCE: THE DOUBLE-EDGED SWORD

In *The Theory of Moral Sentiments*, economist Adam Smith writes, "The great source of both the misery and disorders of human life, seems to arise from overrating the difference between one permanent situation and another."

Adam Smith is asking us to take another look at our own situations and probably saying, maybe it's not that bad. Maybe we are overrating it. Maybe this hopelessness, maybe this terrible situation should be perceived differently. He reminds us that a founder has to disturb the peace of society to achieve their outcomes. "The person under the influence of any extravagant passions, is not only miserable in his actual situation, but is often disposed to disturb the peace of society, in order to arrive at that which he so foolishly admires."

And he adds that "none of them can deserve to be pursued with that passionate ardor which drives us to violate the rules either of prudence or of justice; *or to corrupt the future tranquillity of our minds . . .*" In the quest of innovation and pursuit of extravagant passions, entrepreneurs can make themselves and others miserable. The mantra of persistence is often chanted at the expense of immense sacrifices. Persistence – a noble virtue – can even become a source of misery.

Persistence was my superpower. But now I've come to understand that persistence is a double-edged sword, and my decision not to take a break, to not take more off my plate, hurt me, my family, and the company. That was the biggest mistake of my career.
                        – Ryan Caldbeck, CEO, CircleUp[2]

FOUR TYPES OF STRESSORS

In a survey on emotional resilience conducted by Jonny Miller and Jan Chipchase, the authors found that four types of stressors play out in a founder's life (see Figure 3.1): those driven by external and very precise events (losing a client, shortage of cash), and others driven by internal and ambient triggers (such as imposter syndrome).

Figure 3-1 **Four types of stressors.**

	Specific	
Comparing to others success (triggers feelings of inadequacy)	Losing a major client Cash flow challenges	
Internal ◄		► **External**
Imposter Syndrome	Room temperature Noise levels Poor lighting Air quality	
	Ambient	

Source: Modified from Miller and chipchase 2020

> **Leslie Feinzaig** 🌐
> @LeslieFeinzaig   ...
>
> In my 5 years as an entrepreneur, I've
> paid myself so little that my bank just
> reduced my personal credit limit to
> $350 per month.
>
> 6:24 AM · 3/16/21 · Twitter for iPhone

Source: Twitter, Inc.

Although it may not always be easy to identify the source of our misery, such a framework can be a good starting point.

The external ambient stressors, such as noise, lighting, or air quality may be addressed somewhat easily, but ones that rise on the inside – the internal ambient ones – might be much harder to tackle.

In other situations, our feelings give us a glimpse of our deeper challenges. A feeling of prolonged sadness might be interpreted differently. It could be a symptom of current external circumstances, circumstances in which you have abandoned your own well-being, productivity, or self-worth. Or you may find yourself unable to navigate the demanding routine of work. See Table 3.2.

HOW IS THIS THOUGHT HELPING ME?

External stressors will shake us up, for sure. Even going to a social event for founders can create inane conversational pressures. They will not even let you drink your soju in peace.

Table 3-2 **Internal Feelings versus External Stressors**

Internal Feelings	External Stressors
Sadness – prolonged and heavy	My current circumstances are imposing a cost on me. My desire to seek fitness and well-being is compromised.
Loss of interest in all activities	I do not see the value in doing this activity. I am unable to invest time and effort in anything.
Weight loss / gain, substance abuse	I am unable or unwilling to invest in my own self.
Loss of sleep	My daytime productivity is being traded-off as my cognition seeks a way out of the current crisis.
Anger, frustrations	I am unable or unskilled to navigate my way out of the current crisis. My beliefs, thoughts, or skills are inhibiting me from reaching my goals.
Worthlessness, guilt	My contributions are not valued. I am not delivering on my social contracts. Imposter syndrome.

(*Source:* Table adapted from E. H. Hagen and K. L. Syme, *The Oxford Handbook of Evolution and the Emotions*, Laith Al-Shawaf and Todd Shackelford, eds.).

Christian
@cplans_

At parties, please do not ask what I'm building/if I'm venture backed/ how I will change the world, I really just want to chill and drink my soju in peace :-)

12:36 PM · 7/5/21 · Twitter for iPhone

33 Retweets **6** Quote Tweets **613** Likes

Source: Twitter, Inc.

They do not discriminate, and such is life. Yet, how we react matters. The situation may be the same, but those prone to strong emotional reactions can become far more susceptible to depression. The higher the degree to which a person experiences the world as distressing, threatening, and unsafe, the higher is the probability for a depressive episode. When we are subject to frequent fluctuations of our emotional state – anxiety, tension, and social-withdrawal – researchers term it as neuroticism. See Figure 3.2.

So how should we manage our inner states, and reduce the volatility of our emotions?

Dr. Lucy Hone, who lost her 12-year-old child suddenly, transformed her grief into studies on resilience. She describes one of the most powerful tools in building resilience is to ask,"hmmm . . . and how is this thought/feeling or action helping or hurting me at this moment?"[3]

If our worldview is nonthreatening and safe, we have a four-time lower probability of experiencing a major depressive syndrome. If we see the world differently, change our

Figure 3-2 **Depression and stressful life events.**

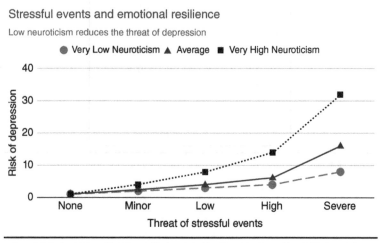

Stressful events and emotional resilience

Low neuroticism reduces the threat of depression

● Very Low Neuroticism ▲ Average ■ Very High Neuroticism

Source: K. S. Kendler, J. Kuhn, and C. A. Prescott, "The Interrelationship of Neuroticism, Sex, and Stressful Life Events in the Prediction of Episodes of Major Depression," *American Journal of Psychiatry* 161, no. 4 (2004): 631–636.

perspective, maybe we can find solace. Selective attention (focus on things you can change, accept the loci of control, making gratitude lists, and so on) is another technique proposed by Dr. Lucy Hone. And finally, a time-tested technique in building resilience is acceptance. Stuff happens. In accepting our setbacks, changing our perspectives and working with thoughts that help, rather than those that hurt us, our start-up ride might be enjoyable.

Which means less misery.

For us.

And for those around us.

4

Obstacles and Frustrations

Competitive dynamics, raising capital, managing cash flows, motivating teams . . . a never-ending stream of obstacles and frustrations, small and big, occur each day.

The scale of problems we face is directly proportional to the size of the opportunity – the game we have chosen to play. When faced with insurmountable obstacles, we often fantasize and design our escape plans. Running away – be it to a beach resort or a meditation camp – seems like a much better option. Numbing ourselves with alcohol, drugs, comfort food, Netflix binges, or other distractions are proven escape mechanisms. The obstacles can cause paralysis, confusion, and it can stall our engines. How can we ensure that the inner balance can be maintained and strengthened at each step?

In looking at the start-up journey, three areas of obstacles and friction arise:

1. The incumbents and legacy companies – the old – will often fight the new. Naturally, these companies have a turf to protect and they would be unwilling to yield.
2. Resources needed – money, people, and time – to reach our goals.
3. Our focus – on gaining rewards versus the process.

BARRIERS TO ENTRY – THE OLD VERSUS THE NEW

When Marc Andreesseen launched Netscape, one of the world's first web browsers, it's adoption rate was meteoric. Netscape owned 90% of the market share and went public, creating wealth and triggering a boom of dot-com innovations. Not to be left behind, Microsoft threw an army of resources and launched Internet Explorer, bundling it for free with existing products and leading to the first browser wars. Netscape was the proverbial David fighting Goliath.

When any new idea is brought into the world, the incumbents will feel threatened and fight back. In start-up jargon, we call it barriers to entry, old versus new, legacy versus upstarts. The validity, utility, or meaning of anything new is questioned, debated, diminished or dismissed. *This has never been done before. It's not a big deal. Why should we care?*

Calcified legacy does not make way for the new easily, nor does it let the new grow or establish roots. Building a product, garnering resources, selling, scaling, negotiating, strategizing – none of this is easy. A battle ensues between the old and new, the legacy and the upstart, the classical versus the modern.

The world fears a new experience more than it fears anything. Because a new experience displaces so many old experiences.

– D. H. Lawrence

The old guard does not want to be displaced. Not so easily and most certainly not without a fight. If start-ups reach any critical mass, the established world feels threatened and will try to crush them. Those in the elite club of entrepreneurship have certainly given up on the mediocre 9-to-5 job. They have appointed themselves as the nonconforming maestros versus the well-adjusted worker bee, the restless loners versus that lazy *hoi polloi*, the ones who see the possibilities versus those who only get stuck with the routine. These two sides – start-ups and incumbents – make enemies of each other, and each side tries to destroy and conquer. This dance filters out the weak, as it mills and grinds and strengthens the new. One popular perspective is that the incumbent is the enemy. The second order view is that having an incumbent, a tough competitor can bring in creativity, speed, and agility.

"The conservative who resists change is as valuable as the radical who proposes it..." writes historian and philosopher Will Durant. "...new ideas should be compelled to go through the mill of objection, opposition, and contumely; this is the trial heat which innovations must survive before being allowed to enter the human race. It is good that the old should resist the young, and that the young should prod the old; out of this tension, as out of the strife of the sexes and the classes, comes a creative tensile strength, a stimulated development, a secret and basic unity, and movement of the whole."

– Will Durant

But often, a formidable competitor can choke the resources of an upstart, create traps, frustrations, and lead the founder down the dark alley, leaving them frustrated and dejected. Marc Andreessen should have been depressed when Netscape was wound down. He probably was frustrated and angry. Getting stalled was an option. Starting his next company was a better option. He focused on what he was good at – the process of building, innovating, and staying ahead of the proverbial curve. He soon started the world's first cloud computing company, Loudcloud. He even went to Detroit to pitch his vision of the next wave of web applications. Loudcloud went public and was acquired by Hewlett Packard (HP). One could argue that if Loudcloud had been around today, it could have been a behemoth like Amazon Web Services (AWS). In the dance of the old and the new, any founder understands that there will be resistance, friction, fistfights. On the inside, the battle between our inner resources and skills versus constraints will define our next step. As a path to resilience, let us look at these two nuances – (i) building resources to overcome constraints (ii) the importance of process over rewards.

RESOURCES VERSUS CONSTRAINTS

The resources we need to leap over obstacles and work around the frustrations fall into two categories, as seen in Table 4.1.

External Resources

- Money, people, and time – never enough of these: Although these boil down into these three simple categories, many founders struggled with their abilities to attract or retain capital. In such situations, their sense of hopelessness is exacerbated.

- Macro-events: As evident in recent times, surging financial markets, political stability, forest fires, social health, and pandemics can create opportunities or constraints. These waves of change drive external events, leading to growth or scarcity of resources.

Table 4-1 **Resources and Constraints Evolve with Stages of Growth**

Stage of Company	Mindset of Core Team	Resources Needed	Constraints
Product Development	Experimentative and flexible	Technical acumen, ability to test assumptions within relevant market segments	Market resistance to adoption, competitive moves, investors' lack of confidence
Early Sales (from 0 to 1)	Engagement and outreach, comfort and ability to sell a vision of a better tomorrow, tenacity, resilience, capacity to handle rejection	Early adopters and design partners, ability to hire sales teams, marketing budgets for customer development and category creation	Stability of product, depth and breadth of features, lack of pricing precision, trade-offs between market segments, go-to-market prioritization
Rapid Growth and Scaling (from 1 to 10)	Competitive, speed and return on investment (ROI) orientation.	Favorable macro trends, repeatable sales efficiency, financial performance, development of brand, competitive strategy and category leadership	Ability to raise capital, hire pro teams, sustaining competitive advantage, maintaining momentum

Internal Resources

Your mental and emotional resources (or if we may call it psychological quotient) can be defined as a combination of the following:

- Mind and body: A founder's state of mind and how they see the world and react to situations are some of the most important resources for any company, yet they are seldom understood or managed effectively.

- Self-view and worldview: How we see the world and our role in it plays an important role in the way we react to situations. If you perceive yourself as able, skillful, and adept, the mastery of situations becomes easier, leading to emotional resiliency. If you perceive the world as overwhelming, with too much to do, or a hostile place, it's time to recalibrate.

- Family and friends: The entrepreneur's image of someone working 24/7, singularly focused on his or her goal, ignoring family, and having no friends is often revered and worshipped. Research shows clear correlation between workaholism, anxiety, and depression.

PROCESS VERSUS REWARDS

Founders focused on rewards and outcomes – that big exit, the pot of gold at the end of the rainbow – are often cheered along by every stakeholder. When money rains down on everyone, joy and milder states of delirium set in. But focusing only on the reward, the outcomes alone, is the surest way of creating frustrations.

Although the founders should certainly focus on the outcomes, those who were stalled often described how they got out of their rut. They fell back on their daily rhythms and processes, and *shifted their focus to the process*, the routine.

They showed up each day and tried to stay in the game, to be a part of the process. Founders would often say:

"Today, I will make that one more sales call."

Let me work on something which is not as intense

"Let me show up, try to get a few things done."

Not as easy, or even feasible to muster up the strength to make such self-talk when you are stalled. But showing up each day, even making small steps was a little hack for some. In a world where everyone is focused on the rewards, that grand prize, or the outcome, staying with the process shifted the focus away toward building resilience.

Daniel Patricio @danielpatricio · 13h   ···
Unless you have been a founder, you can't appreciate the battle from 0 to 1.

I can still live the anxiety attack I had at 21. $30k in debt trying to figure out how to build a damn product.

Working in a hyper growth company is hard. The founder's challenge is existential.

♡ 20   ⟲ 30   ♡ 356   ⬆

Source: Twitter, Inc.

One trick founders use is *to treat the small outcomes of the process* as rewards themselves. It shifts the emphasis of the big reward away and brings in closer rewards, which are not necessarily glorious or financial. "I know that raising a financing round means I have to talk to 50 to 75 investors, even more. Instead of getting disappointed each time I hear a 'no' or get ghosted, I would shift the focus away from that conversation and start to look at the big picture. I'd tell myself, with every 'no,' I'm one step closer to finding that 'yes.' It is a numbers game and this mindset helped me to stay with the process. I would take everything personally, get disappointed every time a pitch did not result in a term sheet. But now I treated it more like a probabilities-game and detached my emotions," says a founder. The process came to the rescue. Having small targets; a consistent daily routine and rhythm of work; and self-care through exercise, sleep, eating habits and social inter-actions eased the pain of the unknown. A sense of autonomy and control of one's life in a routine is a good start for the brain, especially when you are in a funk.

In summary, when founders faced constraints leading to frustrations, they found resources, or mind hacks, that gave them the persistence and ability to stay the course.

Part II

Understanding Our Psychology

In which we look beneath our hood to understand our operating system – our egos, desires, logical constructs, and belief systems.

5

Building Our
Psychological Quotient

> *. . . dealing with our emotions and inner worlds is the
> biggest challenge of all.*
>
> *– from* hackernews, *an online forum
> for entrepreneurs*

Just as we have developed a better awareness of Intellectual
Quotient (IQ) and Emotional Quotient (EQ), let us introduce a
concept of Psychological Quotient (PsyQ), in which we make
an attempt to understand and develop our mysterious internal resources. What constitutes a healthy psychological profile,
especially for founders? How can they develop their awareness of psychology and then strengthen their inner core, which
can help us go on to meet any obstacles and tackle our frustrations with flair?

SEEKING A CRAZY KIND OF ADVENTURE

The core tenets of an entrepreneur's psychology are confidence,
optimism, and a sense of adventure. These tenets propel founders to seek problems – and the bigger the problem, the higher
its lure. For that which can be solved easily provide no sense of
wonder, adventure, or heroic overtures, and those are not worthy. And the reward at the end of the journey could be fame,

fortune, power, or glory. No one knows what the reward will be. Nor can we predict precisely the time. How much? And when? This uncertainty and the mystery of it all excites and intrigues, stoking the fire within. So why do we get stalled? Maybe the journey is way too long. Impatience kicks in. Or we get distracted. Or it suddenly seems too hard. Or maybe the ups and downs of the journey cause nausea and we want to get off the boat.

We have desires, ambitions, and goals. But an entrepreneur's goals are often large, magnanimous, unrealistic, impossible, crazy. Everyone is crazy, but the founder is a different kind of crazy – a crazy that stirs the pot and brings about innovation, spurring big changes in society.

An entrepreneur's level of self-confidence is always higher than most, which instills the courage to seek new possibilities, adventure on different lands, and burn their ships when they find fertile grounds.

Psychological Effects

When we get stalled, facing obstacles that suddenly seem monumental, the brain gets triggered in fight-or-flight mode. Stress hormones turn into a steady flow, which in turn impacts our bodies, appetite, sleep, and emotions. Most importantly, it leads to subconscious behavior patterns as we try to deal with our stress. Our cognitive and executive functions pretty much slow down. Our habitual patterns to reduce stress kick in. These patterns can range from eating junk food, alcohol, or substance abuse. This downward spiral renders us ineffective rapidly. When we get stalled, and are unable to make decisions, the negative spiral can take us into a tailspin. When we stay in the paralyzed states for too long, depression sets in and we may not be able to get out of such states. Getting out of it requires awareness, discipline, and consistent efforts. So part of our own psychological inventory is to understand our motivations, patterns of behavior, and the tactics we use when we face obstacles.

Burnout, Overwhelmed, or Depressed – Giving It a Name

The first step in understanding our psychological quotient is to get familiar with the language and terminology. By giving it a name, we look at it squarely in its face, we understand small parts of it, and we take away some of the fear.

"Surely 'depressed ' is one of the most overworked words in American English," writes author and critic Michael Dirda, "Who isn't depressed? Maybe those who are despondent, dispirited, dejected, disconsolate, downhearted, or filled with despair." So what is exactly my state? Am I *depressed* depressed?

Or am I burned out? In her article "It's Just Too Much,"[1] Jill Lepore writes that burnout cannot be distinguished from depression. To be burned out is to be used up, like a battery so depleted that it can't be recharged. Exhaustion, cynicism, and loss of efficacy, guilt, and self-scolding are its defining symptoms. Three out of four people, a whopping 75% are burned out, according to a 2020 study. If everyone is burned out, and has always been, burnout is just ". . . the hell of life," she writes.

Maybe I am just anxious, stressed, or going through a funky phase? Back in the sixteenth century, *acedia* was described as a state of restlessness, of not living in the present, and seeing the future as overwhelming; it could invade any vocation where the labor is long and the rewards slow to appear, suggests author Kathleen Norris in her book *Acedia and Me*.

That sounds like a good definition of a start-up – the labor is long, the rewards are slow to appear. If I had more money, time, and external resources, would I be able to solve the problems? Or is it due to some unresolved emotions that I am in this state?

When we cannot name the emotions, that makes it harder. When we name the emotions, that might – just might – take away some of their power. The hidden force of the emotions might become a bit bearable. So our first step toward resilience is to call the emotions out.

Figure 5-1 **Acedia - overwhelmed, restless (but not depressed).**

WHEN OUR EMOTIONS CLASH WITH LOGIC

Aristotle proposed this trifecta of logos (reasoning), pathos (emotions), and ethos (ethics), as seen in Figure 5.2, as a way to present the forces inside us.

Our internal landscape is not just composed of logic, like a computer's central processing unit (CPU) with a fantastical clock speed, making amazing decisions at every step of the way. If only it were that simple. We are a smorgasbord of

Figure 5-2 **The trifecta of our inner forces.**

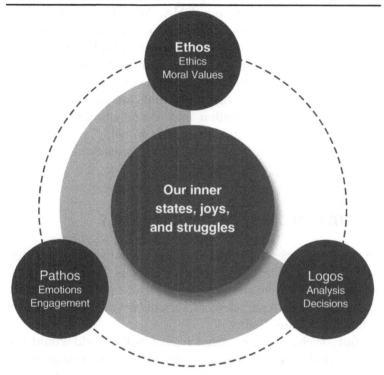

cognitive ability, emotions, desires, dreams, and our fears – our primordial phantasms. All these are loosely coupled together forming our identity – this blob that governs our daily lives and actions. Each of us is like a unique jigsaw of cognitive abilities, emotions, and energy, and these forces can stay aligned, productive, or go against us and create internal rifts.

The rational mind wants to establish its dominance. It is only with reason that we can make progress, it claims. But the heart, the emotional queen – nurturing, caring, loving, and filled with compassion – does not know the voice of reason. It was the broken heart of a mourning Emperor that helped create the magnificent Taj Mahal, one of the Seven Wonders of the World.

Rarely are both these forces – logical and emotional – equally weighted inside our DNA. And if you are heavily weighted in one, you might detest the other. For the emotional, the purely rational mind is much like an inept cold-hearted son-of-a-bitch. For the logically oriented, those full of innocence, love, and cheer are nothing but weak, emotional wimps. The debate rages on. "Emotions and beliefs are masters – reason their servant. Ignore emotion, and reason slumbers – trigger emotion and reason comes rushing in to help," writes author Henry M. Boettinger in his book *Moving Mountains: Or the Art and Craft of Letting Others See Things Your Way.*

THE THREE REGIONS OF INNER CONFLICT

Of course, in a perfect world, each of us would have a wonderful balance of all three elements – emotions, logic, and ethics. We would be able to summon these faculties at the right place at the right time. And, we would attain Nirvana faster than we could spell Gesundheit.

But if such a balance existed in all of us, the world would also be incredibly predictable and boring. This very imbalance creates diversity, adversity, madness, and beauty around us. The rainbow is not just seven colors, but seven billion possibilities.

Whereas logos and pathos are from qualities within, ethics are often brought upon us from without. The external forces impress ethics upon us – our family, religious frameworks, education systems, and our society strive to propose an ethical framework within which we should operate. If you lived alone on an island, ethics would not exist within your daily construct.

As we all know, entrepreneurs are a heady mix of passion, desires, confidence, and optimism. Indeed, these attributes help a company to defy gravitational pull and achieve liftoff. But when an entrepreneur gets stalled, it is mostly due to:

- *Ethics and beliefs* – Do these pull us back or propel us in the right direction?

- *Self-image and our worldviews* – Do our perspectives impact our behaviors and attitudes?
- *Our internal resources* – Do our logical, emotional faculties, courage, and persistence become our superpowers? Or our shortcomings?

Let us unpack these one at a time.

6

Ethics

Ethos – the characteristic spirit of a culture, era, or community as manifested in its beliefs and aspirations . . .
relating to one's character. . .

As a CEO or a founder of a company, it's often upon you to create a code of conduct for the company – this becomes a foundational compass, the North Star and guiding light for the business. Call it an ethical manifesto, such a code helps any team member in making the right choices or doing the right thing – one of the often sprinkled vagaries of modern-day mission statements.

BUILDING A START-UP WITH A SENSE OF MEANING

Ethical codes of conduct are not the first thing on the mind when we optimize for speed and hypergrowth. Let us raise the round of financing, launch the product, get to the first million in revenues – we can work on the ethical codes sometime later, in the future, as we progress. A case in point is Uber, a company that grew faster than any other, yet was beset with ethical conundrums, legal challenges, sexual harassments on its way to becoming a $50 billion juggernaut. It had declared war on, and made an enemy of a taxi-driver. Its goal was to not just to usher in transportation but to destroy the yellow cab. On the path to its initial public offering (IPO) riches, some of its top executives chose to look away and consistently ignore any codes of conduct. The CEO was fired and board members resigned. After the new CEO was ushered in, he went on a year-long *apology tour*.

In a study focused on increasing the *"meaning quotient"* of work, McKinsey research shows that besides focus on the company itself, four other sources give individuals *a sense of meaning*. These include:

1. *Customers* – Value proposition
2. *Team* – A sense of belonging, a caring environment, or working together efficiently and effectively
3. *Yourself as the founder and CEO* – Focus on self-care, personal development, and a sense of empowerment
4. *Society* – How the company leads to a better society, builds the community, or stewards resources

But in start-up land, not all these four drivers of the "meaning quotient" of work play out that well. The relentless focus on customers is a good start and determines the viability of the business itself. Yet often start-up teams are not exactly infused with a sense of belonging. Considered to be stepping stones, people who have been waylaid for their time and skills and disposed of when they are no longer relevant. And the focus on yourself as the CEO is probably the most ignored. A stressed, burnt-out founder, texting on nights and weekends who prides himself on being always on, 24/7, one who rarely focuses on self-care soon might become a sick captain, unable to drive the team toward success. Finally, what is a startup's role in society, beyond the lofty platitudes? And how is that put into practice? With no code, clarity, or direction in creating a fulfilling social order, companies end up becoming soul-sucking machines. Journalist Matt Taibi described Goldman Sachs as an investment bank "wrapped around the face of humanity, relentlessly jamming its blood funnel into anything that smells like money." When ethical frameworks are not prescribed, it's easy to focus on our selfish needs and lose sight of society. Building a better community, being good stewards of resources, maintaining a caring work environment – all these seem like strange apparitions floating in capitalistic lands.

ETHICS, MORALITY, RIGHTEOUSNESS, AND SUPEREGO

Superego. Not the same as ego, but something larger. Ego is more about I, me, myself all the time – living life as a special snowflake. Ego might be a peacock strutting about, splaying out its colorful feathers at all times, brandishing its uniqueness and differentiators. But superego is not quite out there, as loud and bold. It is that soft inner voice of morality, ethics, a higher authority pushing you to "do the right thing," maybe arousing guilt, possibly shame, possibly a perpetually critical parent, or even a board member – always correcting, often criticizing, and never satisfied.

Be it the Ten Commandments or the karmic theory of cause and effect, the superego is glad to remind you to take the high road, act within certain ethical guardrails, failing which we descend into Dante's Inferno of Hell.

Where does the superego come from? How does it permeate into our psyche? And how do our ethical construct and moral values impact our day-to-day activities, our mental health, and well-being? Beginning with our parental influence, the earliest sprinklings of *right versus wrong* establish our baseline. Such views get transmitted over generations, enforcing belief systems, spiritual influences, religion, and social artifacts. As these get embedded into our psyche, our behavior and social interactions are often determined by these hidden lines of code.

Purpose and Mission – The Moral Compass of the Individual and the Company

Based on our backgrounds and worldview, our ethical and moral choices can differ – how we behave, what we eat; some of us are vegan, others kosher. What we see as meaningful, important, and even acceptable wildly differs from one to another. Break the karmic code and, our beliefs say, it will lead to bad times, a falling out, emotional trauma, social ostracism, financial ruin, jail time, penance, or turpitude.

In eastern mythological belief systems, karma plays out across multiple lifetimes. So, yeah, if we screw around big time in this life, we pay over the next eight life cycles. We cannot get away.

Philosophers and pundits have spent their entire lives on ethical debates. How do we determine what is right and what is wrong – morals, and their applications – in our ever-changing lives? This gets especially murky in business where there are no straight answers, nor crisp lines of black and white, just an ample amount of gray.

Letting Ethics Take the Lead

Ethics and superego can establish our guiding principles of behavior. These guidelines – subjective, complex, depending on the circumstances and social order – are often at odds. Within the world of commerce, these can cause immense distress to some and become stumbling blocks; for others, not so much. Indeed, happy are the businesspeople who do not have any moral restraints as they move swiftly, eat, conquer or destroy anything that crosses their way. For such a people, human beings are mere instruments of capitalism; profits and power, their singular goal. When the superego is absent, you fail to look beyond yourself. Take the example of businessman and the former president of the United States, Donald Trump, who was not exactly bound by ethical frameworks. Yet one cannot deny that he was able to achieve his goals – whether it was becoming a real estate mogul, a television star, or presiding at the Oval Office – with dexterity and skill.

But a dominant and a hyperactive superego can become a liability in the world of business. It can reprimand every move, criticize each step. Those who succumb to an overtly rigorous higher order or have a morally righteous superior stance might be prone to dilemmas, deadlocks, setbacks, friction, and frustrations. Amidst the pandemic, even as some businesses struggled, several founders were unsure if they should apply for government loans, called Paycheck Protection Program. Eight hundred billion dollars were being disbursed. While many start-ups would meet the application guidelines, several founders I spoke with felt that a government handout would be morally unacceptable. Others gladly took in as much as they could and celebrated when the government forgave the loans. The inner compass for each of these founders pointed in different directions.

Before my own superego kicks in and points out who is right and who is wrong, let us agree that ethics and morality are complex messy waters in which we wade each day. Yes, these are the building blocks of our code of conduct. But for some, these are our great allies. For others, they just create friction on the path to riches.

How can you let ethics take the lead, before greed takes over?

How does superego cause internal and external conflicts? Let us look at some of the nuances in the following chapters.

7

Do the Right Thing

When it comes to morality and ethics in business, these make strange bedfellows. Most start-ups launch themselves with mission statements that are worthy of being tattooed on the founders' forearms. But these mission statements get altered, adjusted, or deleted as soon as success and big money starts to roll in. And in this crazy dance, a few ground realities prevail. There are no simple answers or easy formulas to appease one and all. Entrepreneurs will be often be beset with ethical conundrums at various stages of growth and inflection points.

ETHICS AT WORK

"We believe strongly that in the long term, we will be better served – as shareholders and in all other ways – by a company that does good things for the world even if we forgo some short- term gains," Google's public offering prospectus proclaimed. When co-founders of Google, Larry Page and Sergey Brin recommended some guiding principles like "don't be evil", then CEO Eric Schmidt thought this was the stupidest rule ever. As he saw it, there's no book that wrote much about evil except maybe, you know, the Bible. Almost 15 years after its IPO, as its market cap grew from $23 billion to over a trillion, Alphabet – Google's parent company – changed their motto from "Don't be evil" to "Do the right thing."

At Uber, all that mattered was growth. Its motto was *win at all costs* and let's make sure archaic concepts like ethics do not mess up that rising trajectory. We can apologize, pay fines, hire lobbyists, litigation attorneys or settle as we march onward to our billions. The company's unfair and unlawful tactics were the subject of multiple blogs, books, and business-school case studies. To choke its competitor, Uber's employees would order and cancel over 5,000 rides, thereby stalling the its business, while trying to recruit away their drivers. Uber's technical achievements included Greyball, a software to thwart city regulators, and Ripley, which automagically locked down computers in the event of any government office raids. Susan Fowler, an Uber engineer, penned a viral blog post describing the culture akin to the wildly popular HBO series *Game of Thrones*, where power, betrayal, and sexual harassment were the norm. None of this mattered to investors. It was an undisputed darling as its valuation grew to nearly $50 billion. Its closest competitor, Lyft's market cap was one-fifth in comparison, but Lyft is hailed as the nicer alternative. After Uber's CEO was ousted and the new CEO, Dara Khosrowsahi came on board, he dropped the "win at all costs" motto from the company's values. He then went on a year-long apology tour engaging with various stakeholders, rebuilding the brand, and often repeating, "We do the right thing. Period."

How should we define the right thing?

GREATEST GOOD FOR THE GREATEST NUMBER

The seventeenth-century English philosopher Jeremy Bentham offered, "The greatest happiness of the greatest number is the measure of right and wrong." That's simple – maximum happiness for maximum number of people. Bentham's maximizing dictum led to the development of utilitarian logic. In business jargon, this could be packaged as cost-benefit analysis. But in business, its effects can be disastrous, especially when shareholder value is unhinged from the moral compass. On one hand, a business can produce products that could have disastrous social consequences. On the other hand, it has to build its own balance sheet and deliver shareholder value. Here is a fine example of a clash of ethics and profits.

When Philip Morris International Inc., famous for its Marlboro cigarettes, decided to launch in Czech Republic, it faced resistance from regulators and political bodies. Citing health challenges and additional public costs incurred due to smoking, the Czech regulators and political bodies were not as eager to let that macho Marlboro Man enter their neighborhood, punch holes in their lungs, run up health costs, or trash cigarette butts all over pretty Prague. Not to be fazed, Phillip Morris hired a management consulting firm, Arthur D. Little, and presented a *cost-benefit analysis* report. The report highlighted the advantages of smoking such as early deaths of citizens leading to significant savings on health care costs and pension payments, offering a net benefit to the Czech government of $30 million each year. See Figure 7.1.

"What an offer – come help us make money on the death of your citizens" was one vitriolic reaction from one Czech resident. Antismoking groups placed ads in the *New York Times*

Figure 7-1 **ROI sans ethics - If the Czechs allowed smoking, the government would make $30 million each year.**

Benefits	Costs
How government can benefit from smoking	**Smoking-related costs**
• Savings on housing for elderly due to early mortality • Pension and social expenses savings • Health care costs savings • Taxes and duties • Income	• Smoking-related health care costs • Public finance/cleanup costs • Fire hazards • Lost income taxes due to mortality

depicting a corpse with a price tag of $1,227. A Czech politician and member of the European Parliament, Libor Rouček remarked, "It is unbelievable . . . ethically unacceptable to think and write about human life in those categories." Czech public health specialist Eva Kralikova suggested sarcastically that under this reasoning "the best recommendation for the government would be to kill all people at the time of their retirement. It's very effective economically." "This is first-class cynicism and hyena-ism," wrote the Czech Republic's leading newspaper, *Mlada Fronta Dnes*, comparing Philip Morris to the Nazi SS. Philip Morris, which has conducted similar studies in other countries, issued a public apology in the *Wall Street Journal*.

In Marlboro country, the superego, which drives ethical values and primary concern for the greater good, was buried under the desire for growth and profits. So what if a few people died along the way! Executives at Philip Morris saw this cost-benefit analysis as the right step toward a boost in the stock price, greater quarterly earnings, and faster year-over-year growth. "Shareholder value," they might chant as they march their way to the bank to deposit their annual bonuses.

Fifty years ago, Philip Morris tried to demonstrate its value proposition and return on investment (ROI) and justify the sale of an addictive product. In modern day, tobacco might have been replaced by social media, which is designed to nurture an addiction, manipulate people and governments, and spread conspiracy theories and disinformation. Social media's effect on mental health and rising teen suicide rates are all treated as a part of the "cost" structure of this ongoing journey to shareholder value creation.

Source: Twitter, Inc.

No matter the product or epoch or the era, shareholder value and greater social good often end up at opposite sides of the table. Balancing these two forces in a capitalistic world is a messy proposition.

ETHICS AND SOCIAL CHANGE – LESSONS FROM COINBASE

For Brian Armstrong, the founder and CEO of Coinbase, it was not an easy task to reaffirm the mission of his company amidst a pandemic, social unrest, and one of the most divisive elections in America. In his blog post, he stated that the company does not engage in broader societal issues unrelated to the company's core mission, because impact comes with focus. Social activism may be well intentioned, but it has the potential to destroy a lot of value at most companies, by both being a distraction and creating internal division. *Even if everyone may agree on the problem, we may not agree on how to solve it.* After this post was published, it stirred up a heated virtual debate and tweetstorms. The company offered generous severance packages to employees who did not agree with the mission of Coinbase. Sixty employees, or 5%, of its team walked out. In his follow-up blog post, the CEO restated that the company does not seek profits alone, but wants to accomplish its mission to create an open financial system in the world and create a great work environment as well.

To put this in context of the superego and ethical dilemmas, consider Coinbase employees who are activists, care about the political environment, and voice their opinions on Twitter and Medium boldly. Their paychecks help them meet the basic needs at the bottom of Maslow's hierarchy of needs. They may struggle with the anger and guilt of being a part of a company that is staying silent – not actively taking a stance in the political debates. Others may not have a strong view and might be ambivalent; they may conclude that the role of the company is to not indulge in politics. Here we see that the superego is not as dominant. Their ego instincts have the ability to resolve such dilemmas. For the ones who feel strongly about politics, a low-level conflict between their superego/ideals and the id/survival needs will lead to frustrations at multiple levels. The ego is stuck somewhere in the middle unable to resolve these opposing forces and find peace between them. If they stay at work, they are unhappy. If they leave, they may find temporary peace, but the survival needs will once again kick in, causing angst at another level.

For Coinbase, that was affirming its culture and values, the work of the superego established clarity amidst chaotic times. The moral compass of the company stayed its course. In writing the post, the CEO's goal was not to seek a unanimous vote of any kind, but to explicitly state what they believed is good for their company, while achieving their broader mission.

The superego in business is all about supporting as many as possible and refraining from hurting others. Can we delay self-gratification, even avoid it for the greater good? Can we invoke our higher selves at all times?

BUILDING AN ETHICAL FRAMEWORK

The design of any ethical framework often starts with the position and perspective of the company and external social conditions. For one, there are no absolutes; while some can be pretty straightforward, others are subjective. And these codes evolve with time and place. Consider the two perspectives in Table 7.1.

An ethical framework is foundational to any business, yet a hyperactive superego, that loud paternalistic voice espousing moral codes and impossible standards of conduct can paralyze a business. A simple example might be offering a bribe. Although it is unacceptable, even illegal, in many parts of the world, the art of the bribe is an essential construct of conducting business. Founders who have a high moral stance will struggle to operate their businesses in such environments, while those who do not have such internal blocks may thrive.

Table 7-1 **An Ethical Framework from Two Perspectives**

Perspective A	Perspective B
Strategy and product design is our primary competitive advantage.	Corporate culture and well-being is our primary competitive advantage.
If we are profitable, only then we can serve our society and higher purpose.	If we follow our higher purpose and serve the society, then profits will follow.
Profits allow society and people to improve and hence, profits come first.	We should focus on people first and profits later; by developing and supporting people, profits happen.
Focus on results.	Appreciate the efforts.
Our organization chart defines our responsibilities to each other.	Our organization chart defines our relationship to each other.
Our hard work determines our performance.	Our well-being determines our performance.
The best offense is a good defense.	The best defense is a good offense.
Our customers are here because of the excellence of our products.	Our customers are here because of who we are and what we do.
Success creates more success. Let's not waste time analyzing modes of failure.	We learn from our failures. Success has many fathers.

In any business, the ethical side (or the superego) of morality might battle the basic needs of survival – namely, cash flow and profitability (or the id). When one side overpowers the other, the ego has lost its ability to balance these two opposing forces. One can lead to hedonistic empires, while the other extremity can cause paralysis of moral and value conundrums, battling commercial interest. As one founder told me bluntly, "The place of business is no different from warfare. I have no place for high priests pontificating values at every step of the game – I only need warriors to join my team."

The practical challenges of running a business are far too numerous. Although morality and ethical order have their foundational place, they need to be blended with the rational and the rules of the marketplace. In the case of Coinbase, the CEO could have lost his way by taking a populist stance. Or, by staying silent, he could have ignored the debate and buried his head in the sand. Yet he took the challenge head on, declared his position offered a severance for those who had a different perspective, and moved on. At the appointed hour, a strong ego can balance the needs of the business and the demands of superego.

The drive for profits is the basic purpose of a corporation and individual well-being is not featured in the corporate charter. As Freud and other psychological experts have reminded us, the adept ego, one that can effectively negotiate between the *morally superior pull of the superego and the drag of the hedonistic id* can emerge as the winner in the game of business. If the superego muzzles the ego down with righteousness and establishes moral standards that are nigh impossible to address, it may be hard to run a business. On the other hand, if desires run amok and the ego is unable to curtail impulses, we have a weak flighty operator, getting swayed by the wind.

All our developmental efforts should focus on making the ego strong, compatible, and nimble.

But how do you do that?

Albert Einstein Invokes the Superego

Concern for the man himself and his fate must always form the chief interest of all technical endeavors; concern for the great unsolved problems of the organization of labor and the distribution of goods in order that the creations of our mind shall be a blessing and not a curse to mankind.

Never forget this in the midst of your diagrams and equations.
— Albert Einstein, from a speech to students at the
California Institute of Technology, in "Einstein Sees
Lack in Applying Science," New York Times
(February 16, 1931)

8

Ego – The Emperor and the Slave

*Your thoughts, and your identification with your
thoughts is your ego. You start to believe in every
thought that arises, and you derive your sense of who
you are from these thoughts. Thoughts can get stuck
in our heads, become deeply lodged in our minds and
we start to believe in them. Then this becomes your
ego – it is an entity, not apart from your thoughts.*

– Eckhart Tolle

What is this thing called the ego? Is it an artifact, a glorified self-portrait that we draw and redraw for the rest of our life? Where does it come from? An infant or a child does not have an ego. Nor does a sick, dying person. Appearing mysteriously as we start adulting and abandoning us silently toward the end of our lives, our egos build their identity and foundation and whip its appetite for distinction for much of our lives. Building on the functioning of our minds, our thoughts, and the social order, our egos can be both our best ally and our worst enemy. Freud defined ego as follows:

"The ego functions to categorize things and persons in the outside world (those with whom I identify versus those with whom I conflict), but even more importantly the ego discriminates between contending forces of my own desire (impulses on which I will act versus those I will refuse and repress)."[1] Author Adam Phillips writes, "We are, at some basic level of ourselves, a chaos of conflicting urges. Ego refers to the restricted economy of impulse that grounds my feeling of having a stable and predictable identity. The ego selects from a range of impulse energies and leaves the others behind."[2]

Our desire to be different and be better than others can be an impetus for progress. Innovations occur and beautiful music and soulful experiences arise when we aspire to be better and different. For, it is our ego that helps us in developing our potential. The ego defines our own image and how we see the world; both have strong imperatives in how we navigate tough situations.

> *Self image:* How we see ourselves – as capable or confused, as adept or inept, as glorious or shameful, as persistent and strong or weak
>
> *Our worldview*: How we see our circumstances, others and engage with those around us – as rational adults, peace loving humans, or as stupid, overbearing maniacs, greedy monsters or weaklings

IMPULSES, EGO, AND SUPEREGO

The Greek philosopher, Plato draws an image of winged horses and their charioteer. He writes, in his book *Phaedrus*, "To begin with, our driver is in charge of a pair of horses; second, one of his horses is beautiful and good and from a stock of the same sort, while the other is the opposite and has the opposite sort of bloodline. This means that chariot driving in our case is inevitably a painfully difficult business." Our various desires yank us in different directions and the charioteer – our ego – is trying to navigate the way, keeping those desires aligned toward a destination that only she can see. Furthering this similar concept of the soul, Freud writes, "The horse supplies the locomotive energy, while the rider has the privilege of deciding on the goal and of guiding the powerful animal's movement. But only too often there arises, between the ego and the id, the not

Figure 8-1 **The ego, the superego, and the id: The emperor, the salve, the negotiator of all things.**

Super Ego	• Ethics and Moral Values / Do's and Don't • "If you are good, you will go to Heaven"
Ego	• Adaptable Adult / Get this done • "Let's figure out a way to work with each other"
Id	• Impulses, Desires, Gratification • "I want this right now or else I will cry"

precisely ideal situation of the rider being obliged to guide the horse along the path by which it itself wants to go."

Freud identified the three elements of our psyche – the id, the ego, and our superego (see Figure 8.1). Our id is what drives us to seek fulfillment of our basic needs. Food, sleep, bodily needs and demands, including our sexual drive is tied to our id. Freud called it a cauldron of seething excitations, filled with energy. In our id, competing forces and contradictions exist side-by-side. One part of us wants something and another part holds us back. Our id does not offer value judgments or moralistic views of what is right and wrong. A baby is filled with id, as a delightful ball of flesh; it is cute but works only with instinctual needs. The ego, in Freud's view, is like our id's big brother, more mature and adult-like. It is a modified version of our baser instincts. It takes the id's primal drives and brings some management to the chaos. The ego assigns priorities to the incessant urges, demands, and drives, and delays, regulates, or gratifies our id in creative ways. If the id is pure passion, the ego is the voice of reason. The ego dethrones the pleasure principle of life and helps us to stay organized. Between these two, there is a tension – a give-and-take – and negotiations happen at all times. While the ego stands for reason and good sense, it must also carry out the id's intentions and cannot simply ignore them. It must find the best circumstances in which the id's goals can also be achieved. Neither the ego nor the id can be fully in control. "Human beings fall ill of a conflict between the claims of an instinctual life and the resistance which arises against it," he wrote. Comparing our id and our ego to a horse and its rider, Freud suggested that the rider (or the ego) needs superior strengths, drawn from the external world around us. This allows us to manage our baser instincts.

Finally, the superego is one step higher than the ego and often is an ideal self. The superego is often crafted by early influences of our parents, teachers, gurus, priests, or philosophers. All those who instilled tradition, values, culture, wisdom, religion, and ideals have helped shape our superego. The superego is also the voice of our inner critic, making judgment calls. According to Freud, the superego is the vehicle of tradition, representative of moral restrictions, steadily propagating from generation to generation. Yet the superego makes a one-sided choice by picking only the stricter side of our parents, with a strong prohibiting and punishing function. Guilt is nothing but the tension between our ego and the superego. The superego applies the strictest moral standards to the ego, often abuses, humiliates, and ill-treats our ego, threatening it with punishment and reproaching it for actions of the remote past. *"The way our superego treats the ego can lead to depression,"* suggests Freud.

And, for those of us who get enamored by a morally superior stance in life driven by the superego, Freud warned that "we ought not to exalt ourselves so high as to completely neglect what was originally animal in our nature. Our civilized standards make life too difficult for the majority of human organization."

WHY IS EGO NECESSARY IN BUSINESS?

A well balanced ego is the necessary carrier of the gift of the soul.
— Bill Plotkin, psychologist and author of
Soulcraft: Crossing into the Mysteries of Nature and Psyche

A healthy ego is essential to keep the horses aligned, to survive, thrive, and serve the society. It helps us care and provide for our families, develop our ideas despite pushbacks, innovate and execute our plans, and stand strong when winds blow. It gives us direction; channels our drive, conviction, an inner sense of strength, persistence; and does not let us get destabilized. All progress depends on a healthy ego. If Michelangelo, Galileo, and Newton did not have healthy egos, the Sistine Chapel would be a boring place, the laws of gravity would not be propounded, and the Flat Earth Society's membership would have grown to an all-time high. Those who have mastery of social order, are aware of the rules of the game, can participate in the game of commerce, meet their own needs with panache without missing a beat, and hold their head high have healthy egos.

THE EGO AND OUR SELF-IMAGE

As we perceive the path ahead and the world around us, the ego helps us to interact with the world. It allows us to work within a given set of opportunities and constraints, deploy our skills, and progress toward our goals. The ego is our ally in that it allows us to do our duty, engage in society, give and receive goods and services, transact and exchange value efficiently. One way to think about the ego is like that of a conductor of a symphony in our daily life. The musicians – like our senses – have to be rested, well fed, and tuned to do their parts with the range of their instruments. If the audience is full of fearfully giant demons, the conductor can unleash the horn section and blast them away. If little babies are in the audience, the symphony is directed to turn on the caring viola and the lullabies. As life throws challenges at us, our ego reacts, juggles, twists, and turns with the rhythms, and sometimes, when it gets too much, it can lose its balance. Some days it gets overwhelmed. We get tired and give up. On other days, it can dance a beautiful dance. We feel like we are at our productive best.

Two Contrasts in Self-View: Frank Lloyd Wright and Eileen Fisher

Frank Lloyd Wright: World's greatest architect

Architect Frank Lloyd Wright once said, "Early in life, I had to choose between honest arrogance and hypocritical humility. I chose honest arrogance and have seen no occasion to change." He once was called on to testify at a trial. When he was asked to identify himself on the witness stand, he answered, "Frank Lloyd Wright, the world's greatest architect."

Asked later why he responded that way, Wright said, "I was under oath."

Having designed over 1,000 structures, which integrated the organic design of natural elements, members of the American Institute of Architects named his work Fallingwater the "best all-time work of American architecture."

Compare Frank Lloyd Wright's views and self-image with those of entrepreneur Eileen Fisher.

Eileen Fisher: Just an ordinary person

I know the idea for the company came through me in some way, but it's beyond me. I planted the first seed, and now I look around and there is this beautiful amazing garden. But I'm just an ordinary person . . . being treated as special feels a little weird to me.

– Eileen Fisher, founder of a retail clothing company. Eileen started the company over 30 years ago. The privately held company generates about $300 million in revenues.

Our ego also feeds on our innate desire to be differentiated and stand tall from all those around us. And the entrepreneurial ego is anything but normal. The stronger the ego, the more skillful the founder is in navigating the murky terrains. The artists, sports athletes, and scientists stretch themselves to gain appreciation, attention, gold medals, and Nobel Prizes. The ego creates an image of ourselves – sometimes overinflated, sometimes hypercritical, but rarely objective. Narcissus loved his image too. Cheering us along at every step, as unique, invincible, and omnipotent, our ego separates us from the rest of society. This image of our self occurs gradually by a series of steps. First our education (I'll take ivy league, thank you) then our skills (a member of Mensa club, maybe), our social connections (elite), our titles at work (CEO), the corner office (with a view) or communal spaces, the cars we drive (Teslas or Lamborghinis), and the neighborhoods in which we live (best part of town). We spend an extraordinary amount of time in our lives trying to first build an image, and then do our best to hang on to this construct. But, this image largely exists in our own minds and is often the central theme in most dramas that occur in our life.

Those who are stressed, exhausted, anxious, and depressed often find their self-views – how they perceive their own strengths – as inadequate. For them, the first step is to resurrect their own selves. The ego lies deflated and needs to be propped up.

9

Working with Your Ego

The first half of life is devoted to forming a healthy ego, the second half is going inward and letting go of it.

– C.G. Jung

To not only acknowledge and accept our ego as our ally, but to understand it and work with it – that may well be our biggest challenge.

Not to pretend it doesn't exist, nor to debase it. Not to abhor it, nor to fight it. Not to assume a self-righteous, superior stand by pointing it out in others, with statements like "that guy's ego is bigger than his brains."

The ego is in all of us. It helps us. And it is distorted for most of us. The Dalai Lama has an ego and so does the communist czar of China. The janitor has an ego and so does the chairman of the board.

If being an egomaniac means I believe in what I do and in my art or music, then in that respect you can call me that . . . I believe in what I do, and I'll say it.

– John Lennon

Beware of mystics and philosophers who urge you to negate your ego and annihilate it completely. That is all very good if you seek a spiritual path and a monastic life in the mountains. In the world of business, you absolutely need your ego, but as a faithful ally – and a strong wingman. One that will help take the reins and navigate your journey skillfully through stormy weather, making sure the plane does not crash. A healthy ego guides us toward stability, skillful management of life, and financial independence. First the ego should help stabilize your own position. And then strive to rise above to serve others. This can be much harder as philosophically, the very power that helps you differentiate cannot then help you embrace, commune, or empathize.

An ego that becomes your greatest ally and, eventually, excels in serving others for the rest of your life is a healthy ego, because, as Carl Gustav Jung writes, "Only a life lived in a certain spirit is worth living. It is a remarkable fact that a life lived entirely from the ego is dull not only for the person himself but for all concerned."

But no school teaches us how to work with this mysterious part of ourselves. How do we work with this abstract yet integral force within us? We have been told that our egos do more harm than good. Is it so? Like love of money, it is to be treated as the root of all evil. However, it's not money but lusting after the excess that foments the evil. In the same way, we might say that an ego that lusts solely after its own self image is an unhealthy ego.

A FOUNDER'S EGO IS ABNORMAL

A founder's ego is stronger than most, as it does not accept the status quo. It does not quietly adjust to the social environment and try to please everyone. In fact, it's quite the opposite. The founder's ego wants to establish its presence or, to put it in entrepreneurial lingo, to make a dent in the world. Such an ego is a gift to society when it functions skillfully and achieves its objectives. Innovators, entrepreneurs, scientists, and philosophers who navigate the tricky terrains of their domains and rise above have used their abnormal ego to change the status quo – sometimes gently, sometimes with force.

We should welcome this abnormal force, only if we first establish the purpose –a purpose for greater good. We often start to assemble our technological tools, raise money, and hire people in this rush to make a dent in the world quickly. Time is of the essence, and boy, are we in a hurry to get somewhere! But time spent on soul-searching and finding your own purpose is time well spent. To build a solid foundation for your ego is time well spent.

WHO DOES YOUR EGO SERVE?

Compare the ego of an established entrepreneur like Jeff Bezos or Elon Musk. Here you have an ego that sets an agenda, boldly navigates its way across a wide range of problems – people, money, markets, and competition. Even outer space. It achieves outcomes we could never fathom, and plows on each day, vanquishing its enemies. In contrast, the ego of a maniacal politician serves himself alone, as he is bent on seeking attention, grabbing power, and creating divisions in society all along the way.

If our egos are about narcissistic focus on ourselves all the time, the cracks begin to appear. Our egos are only too glad to help. But they should help as many as possible, and not just us. Gandhi had an ego, and so did Hitler. Their individual pursuits of peace versus power were their only difference.

If there's anything more important than my ego around, I want it caught and shot now.
    – Douglas Adams, The Hitchhiker's Guide to the Galaxy

Our ego can manifest itself in service of our incessant desires, needs, and greed, or it can rise to serve many. We become hamsters in a never-ending money-making cycle, or we can serve a larger part of our society.

The ego is the engine, brimming with horsepower.

The superego is the compass, showing the direction.

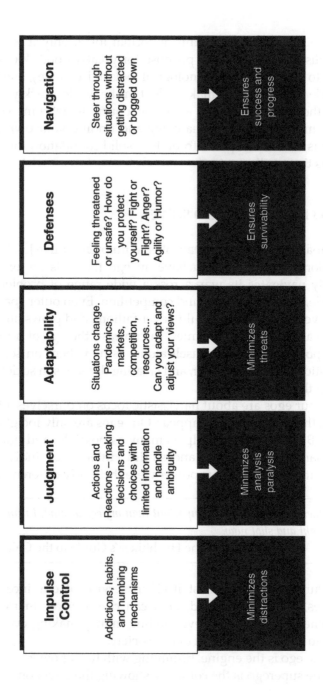

THE EGO IS NOT THE ENEMY

The ego is not the enemy, but an overinflated ego could become one, where the sense of self-importance is inflated or we are lacking in purpose or authenticity.

A gigantic ego, says Hafiz, will keep you busy with worries and bills, and won't give you much time to sing in this world. We then become angry, greedy, hurtful, aggressive, aggravated . . . In Nobel laureate Rabindranath Tagore's lament, we find our own ego's swagger.

> *I came out alone on my way to my tryst.*
> *But who is this that follows me in the silent dark?*
> *I move aside to avoid his presence but I escape him not.*
> *He makes the dust rise from the earth with his swagger;*
> *he adds his loud voice to every word that I utter.*
> *He is my own little self, my lord, he knows no shame;*
> *but I am ashamed to come to thy door in his company.*
>
> *Rabindranath Tagore*

Yet if we can master our egos, and gradually make them of service to many, we can find solace in the fact that we are indeed an instrument of change. Bertrand Russell urges us to *make our interests gradually wider and more impersonal, until bit by bit the walls of the ego recede.* As the mystics say, an individual human existence should be like a river: small at first, narrowly contained within its banks, and rushing passionately past rocks and over waterfalls. Gradually the river grows wider, the banks recede, the waters flow more quietly, and in the end, without any visible break, they become merged in the sea, and painlessly lose their individual being.

A Gigantic Ego

-Hafiz

The only problem with not castrating
A gigantic ego is
That it will surely become amorous
And father
A hundred screaming ideas and kids
Who will then all quickly grow up
And skillfully proceed
To run up every imaginable debt
And complication of which your brain
Can conceive.
This would concern normal parents
And any seekers of freedom
And the local merchants nearby
As well.
They could very easily become forced
To disturb your peace;
All those worries and bills could turn to
Wailing ghosts.
The only problem with not lassoing
A runaway ego is
You won't have much time to sing
In this sweet world.

10

The Hidden Land of Desires and Motivations

A creative man has no choice. He may come across his supreme task almost accidentally. But once the issue is joined, his task proves to be at the same time intimately related to his most personal conflicts, to his superior selective perception, and to the stubbornness of his one-way will; he must court sickness, failure, or insanity in order to test the alternative whether the established world will crush him, or whether he will disestablish a sector of this world's outworn fundaments and make place for a new one.

– Erik H. Erickson, psychologist

MEET YOUR ID

All the basics that we need – food, sleep, bodily needs, and demands, including our sexual drive, come from our id. When you are having a good day, the desires have been satiated. The id is happy and content. Often, the id the first one inside us to acknowledge a good day.

Id is where our impulses, desires, competing forces, and contradictions coexist; all these exist side by side in this bubble called id. Our id does not offer value judgments or moralistic views of what is right and wrong. It just asks for what it needs – immediately and bluntly. And it wants everything here and now. A baby is filled with id, as a delightful ball of flesh, cute and driven by instinctual needs of food, sleep, and a wet diaper. When we grow up, the id manifests itself in a storm of desires – sometimes essential needs, other times mindless addictions.

Once the basic desires are met, we inch upward to try something bigger – such as attempting a start-up or mining asteroids.

THE DESIRE TO START SOMETHING UP

Mediocrity "is the refusal to let the inner brilliance shine. The way of life, its expression and values…," writes author Thomas Moore. And in Silicon Valley, the propensity to amplify their inner brilliance is omnipresent. Infused with mantras of "think different" or "think Big," founders are not merely searching for the equivalent of a game-changing Mt. Everest of a problem. They want to put a lasso around asteroids, build satellite cubes, store blockchain records in ether, beam internet signals from space, or – the final exit strategy – get out of Earth and inhabit Mars. These are problems that very few would even dare to conceive, let alone aspire to. The range of technical and economic resources or courage of spirit is simply not available with the vast majority. And if perchance some did aspire to, only a minute fraction would eventually attempt.

Reaching for the Stars – Scale of Ambition

Several years ago, at a fine wine and cheese event at the Rosewood Hotel on Sandhill Road in Silicon Valley, I met a founder of a rather unconventional company – an asteroid mining start-up. It was one of those dating events during which founders and investors mingled, each one trying to find their best catch of the evening. But such events often stretch the limits of the possible. It's the entrepreneurs who do the stretching, while investors like me stay dumbstruck, either in awe, confusion, or wonder. In Silicon Valley, solving problems that an average Joe can tackle is passé and not worthy of cocktail conversations. If mediocrity is doing only what is necessary and sufficient – a regular 8-to-5 work routine – founders are anything but mediocre.

Why do you want to chase asteroids? I mean, there are so many other immediate urgent and pressing problems you could solve, I asked. This look on the founder's face was that of a wise father looking down upon a wayward, clueless child. I sensed that he pitied me for my lowlife question. To show me the light, his brilliant light, he had a well-rehearsed script of an elevator pitch, rife with passionate overtures, missionary zeal, and marketing speak:

As a child, I was heavily influenced by [I don't remember exactly but fill in the blank . . . Isaac Asimov, Carl Sagan, Sputnik, Star Wars . . .] and when at 12, I got my first [again . . . something like Atari, Apple computer/telescope/microscope], I started to wonder . . .

Soon I realized I was in the presence of a modern-day Mozart or Mahler – child prodigies of their own merit – who were composing magnificent overtures, but just with code. The arrangement and rearrangement of the bits and bytes, people, and capital was elegant, minimal, efficient, and lean. And instead of the Ninth Symphony's climactic cacophony of trumpets and cymbals, rising to thunderous applause, the exit here was no longer an IPO or a financial windfall. It was actually an exit from this f**king planet. I had too many questions, but the first one was how soon can I exit from this crazy conversation. The second one was where such do such desires and motivations come from.

The Second-Order Effects as a Motivator – Looking Beyond the Financial Returns

Later that night, in my mildly drunken stupor, I Googled my way into the investment merits of asteroid mining and it came as no surprise that Larry Page, founder of Google, and Eric Schmidt, the former CEO of Google had already invested in this company. Investing in moon shots was *de riguer*, and this was magnificent in scale and aspiration. Asteroids fly at speeds upward of 15,000 miles per hour. To find the right one, latch onto it, dig around to see what it is made up of, extract the elements and bring it back home . . . what a messy, complex monster of a problem. The thrill, the infinite engineering challenge that such a project would bring. Sending a man to the moon pales in comparison and sounds like a kindergartner's toy project. That's for the boys. This is for the real men. Estimates from NASA put the cost of mining any asteroid at about a billion dollars. It would be just like poking around the earth's basin for oil wells, except this would be a bit out there. A few more moving parts, gravitational forces not included. If we are lucky, we might find precious metals – say platinum or gold. The average yield, if we find a good, rich asteroid, might be up to two kilos. On the London Metal Exchange, platinum fetches $30 per gram and gold is roughly twice that amount (at the time of writing this book). Which means each mission, which would cost a billion dollars, could make roughly $100,000. If the estimates are in any way accurate, that is like spending $10,000 to get one dollar back.

But, never mind the meager return on investment (ROI) and my myopic view of economic inputs and outputs. A few years later, as I was finishing up this manuscript, the following news was published:

Hubble telescope identifies an asteroid, Psyche, made of metal – the value of iron alone on the asteroid was estimated to be worth approximately $10,000 quadrillion, which is more than the entire economy of the World. Researchers said that they do not plan to bring any of its metal back.

Source: CBS News, October 18, 2020

The entrepreneurial empires were not built purely on ROI. It's the monster of a fight that invokes the founder's spirit. The abnormal ego needs an abnormal problem. The founders have decided to solve such a complex problem, so far-fetched that their sanity might come under scrutiny. The CEO of Google had endorsed this company, writing a check, egging such a founder on. I'm sure he did not endorse the idea to go grab a few asteroids before lunchtime. Nor did he visualize that Apple commercial celebrating the crazy ones.

He was fueling the founder's insatiable appetite to develop complex problem-solving skills. Any money made would be a nice byproduct. But if no money came out of this experiment, the investor would have helped a ninja-team build some very intricate problem-solving muscles. When we think about the vast range of skills needed to solve such complex problems, it's only then that we can even begin to celebrate the crazy ones. Rocket propulsion, mathematics, physics, metallurgy, and mining – all of these applied to solve a grand problem that has never been solved before. If we maintain the pragmatic view, and do not see beyond the surface, we fail to see the second order benefits of such experiments. We throttle the founders' spirit and inhibit the future, a spirit that aches to blossom with new possibilities. Our society would benefit, one way or another as these founders build their technical muscles. I promised myself never to ask stupid questions again.

OUR HIDDEN DESIRES AND DRIVERS

One perspective is that these crazy-rich entrepreneurial megalomaniacs are trying to disrupt everything, get rich quick, and establish global dominance. Or another way of looking at it is how can we experiment and innovate on the existing form of political governance? For sure, those in power corridors of Washington, DC, have no incentive to make any changes, as in any other land of incumbents. When the old guard does not let the new order arise, we might have a problem. Bill Gates wants to solve energy problems and health care challenges at a grand global scale. His push for nuclear-power-generation technologies, those that are clearly far-more superior, could even eliminate the 90,000 metric tons of nuclear radioactive waste being stored in the United States. But these innovations have yet to see the light of the day, and have not been adopted due to incumbents and politics. These barriers surely keep him up at night as he fights the good fight each day. The romantic in me absolutely loves the idea of using our time, money, and intellectual resources in experimenting with grand problems. The pragmatist in me fails to see the utilitarian value, when so many are dying of hunger.

- What pushes one person to try and mine asteroids, or inhabit Mars, while others are content with simpler 9-to-5 lives?
- What gives one immense striving for the impossible, the magical?
- What causes such restlessness, how does one gather tenacity, fortitude, and spirit to take on these challenges and never stop till they scale their self-established summits?

One theory we could postulate is that the bigger the hole in your psyche, the grander the problems we seek. In seeking such problems, we find our own sense of purpose. Feeding the hungry is important, but it does not address my own hunger; it might bring me peace but it does not help my psyche, some hidden need that I cannot fully articulate – a need of love, of fame, of fortune, of more attention, of social validation, of recognition, of approval.

Our desires might come from within or they can be triggered from external signals. We often want what others want. And as silly as it may be, we can do mindless stuff just to keep up with the social order.

Desires – Intrinsic and Extrinsic

Most of us are gooey lumps of desires and fears. All our quests are toward pleasure, or more so, a sense of contentment. The mind loves pleasurable feelings, gets addicted to the rush, and tries to recreate those feelings over and over again. Such feelings might be of the body – food, clothing, jewelry and accouterments, money, and other material aspects. Some feelings are triggered by substances. Others come from feelings of love, affirmations, approvals, nurturing, and caring relationships. As basic needs are met, our desires start to propel us in newer terrains. The desire for social approval, respect, power, and fame can push us on magical quests.

Yet, where do desires come from? The founder's desire to start a business can be intrinsic or driven by external motivations.

In Silicon Valley, everyone wants to have their own start-up, just as everyone wants their own Tesla, vineyard, or microbrewery (depending on your taste). An entrepreneur could start a company no sooner than she has spotted an opportunity. But it could also be an escape from boredom, a way to stay busy, to mask the stigma of unemployment, or a vain attempt to seek an entry into the hallowed halls of entrepreneurial clubs – a social validation. How does our social environment shape our desires? How do we navigate some desires and avoid others?

THE DANGER OF UNMET DESIRES

All the other kids have a start-up . . . and I want one too.

In one of his shareholder letters, Warren Buffett shines a light on the fundamental trigger of human desires – we want something because others have it. We don't want to be left out. "Some years back, a CEO friend of mine – in jest, it must be said – unintentionally described the pathology of many big deals. This friend was explaining to his directors why he wanted to acquire a certain type of a company. After droning rather unpersuasively through the economics and strategic rationale for the acquisition, he abruptly abandoned the script. With an impish look, he simply said: 'Aw, fellas, all the other kids have one.'"

Michael Seibel
@mwseibel

I've noticed that many people compete in games they don't understand because they are modeling the behavior of people around them. Most common is the competition for wealth as a proxy for happiness.

1:45 PM · 6/22/19 · Twitter Web App

504 Retweets **78** Quote Tweets **2,027** Likes

Source: Twitter, Inc.

We all know founders who start companies because one of their friends started a company, and they also want one of their own. A friend got accepted in an accelerator program and soon you also apply, because why not? Like a toy, or that nice new car in the neighborhood, our desires are often triggered externally. This is not all that bad. The idea, the inspiration can come from anywhere. Facebook was not Mark Zuckerberg's idea nor was Google the first search engine. Musk did not start Tesla. I could extend this notion, somewhat fantastically, that the idea for SpaceX might have been triggered in Musk's head by Arthur Clarke, who said, just as Musk was exiting PayPal,[1] "The dinosaurs became extinct because they didn't have a space program. And if we become extinct because we don't have a space program, it'll serve us right!"

In 1897, Oscar Wilde wrote to one of his friends lamenting, "Most people are other people. Their thoughts are someone

else's opinions, their lives a mimicry, their passions a quota-
tion." Our ability to imitate, often subconsciously, is well established over the ages. "People know what they want because
they know what other people want," writes German psychologist Theodor Adorno.

Our desires are shaped by what we see around us. In many
conversations, I find founders asking for the same premoney
or exit valuation that was announced in the media last week.
Often this is not hinged upon the realities of each one's unique
business model, its progress, growth, market conditions, or
competitor dynamics.

René Girard writes that "the real founders of capitalism are
monkeys." Capitalism gives our desires free rein to spread and
grow in our society. This can cause a crisis of sorts, he warns.
As desires spread in our society, we unleash the contagion in
different domains, which leads to an irreversible escalation.
"The price for all this is perhaps neuroses," warns Girard. "The
value of the object we desire grows in proportion to the resistance met with in acquiring it."

Desires lead to demands. Resources are limited. Competition
grows to meet demands. If demand outstrips supply, the scarcity can pit us against one another, creating rivals, fights, and
wars. If supply outstrips demand, with a bunch of me-toos,
prices drop, margins drop, and the weak companies die. The
cycle of desire primes the pump for the economic cycles.

The Internet of Things Your Mom Won't Do
for You Anymore

Consider, for instance, the start-up that promises to do your
laundry by connecting you to local laundromats or get you
food in real time by connecting you with local chefs. Laundry
and cooking may be tasks that software engineers would rather
not do themselves, but platforms haven't made these chores
any easier to deal with. They're what our friend Pierre Azou-
lay, an economist at MIT's Sloan School of Management, calls
"the Internet of things your mom won't do for you anymore."

Source: Piai / Adobe Stock

In this world of externally triggered desires, those founders who have crisp and clear inner callings are fortunate indeed. For the spark inside is lit by an unknown power. Their ability to stay on their paths, be persistent, and press-on is remarkably different. Elon Musk once famously said, "It is very difficult to start companies – I have one piece of advice that may sound discouraging. *If you need inspiring words, don't do it.*"

But most of us are not as resilient as Musk, and we occasionally fall apart. Our inner spark may sputter, and on some days, not blaze as strong. That is why discipline, building a schedule, a routine, and daily muscle is important. But before we get into all that daily routines, disciplines, and such, let us understand how our minds process our desires, while battling 18 other impulses and distractions at the same time.

A World of Want

-by Tina Schumann

I tried to imagine each life.
Not so much where they were
going, but what they were made of:
wounds, illusions, desires, deceits...
Through all of this a preoccupation
with the next perceived need floats-up
like thought bubbles inside my head:
Coffee, Cheetos, sex, a new blouse, a larger house,
a desk fan, appreciation from that one specific person,
the phones chirp, the trip to France.
If I could quiet this conga-line of cravings
what lingering longings would I lament?
What radiant unattached insights
would I muster? Who would I be
without my constant yearnings?
It's a world of want. You get the idea.

11

Logos and the Mind

What a strange machine man is!
You fill him with bread, wine, fish, and radishes,
and out comes sighs, laughter, and dreams.

– Nikos Kazantzakis

Quite magical, aren't we, this human being, this body and mind? But ask anyone, what is a mind?

THE ANALYTICAL ENGINE OF THE MIND

Is it a machine for processing our logical faculties or *logos*? Does it make important decisions and calculating trade-offs? Does it navigate desires, such as aim for world peace and keep us from eating flaming Cheetos for breakfast? Indeed, the mind is a mysterious machine that moves seamlessly across time – between the present moment and the past experiences. It inspires the future fantasies, fears, and desires. It is constantly trying to juggle between the axis of time and pleasure/pain rollercoaster rides. It creates fantasies that can make us delirious with joy or crippling anxieties. The past can bring a rush of pleasant feelings or suck us into a whirlpool of sadness. The mind takes us for a ride, all day every day to all these corners. But what about staying in the present? Ah – that, my friends, is tough for the mind. The mind does not stay in the present (see Figure 11.1) because it slows down the engine – the flitting bird has to sit still, with nothing to chew on.

Figure 11-1 **The mind across time.**

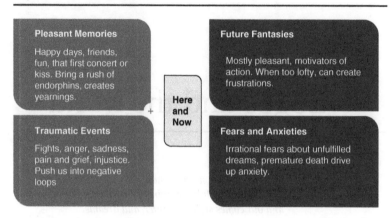

How do we develop the mind – its faculties? How do we become stronger in certain mental strengths? What gives us the dexterity to keep moving in life and what causes us to give up, throw our hands up in despair? Our biological, temperamental, social, and philosophical realms may impact our cognitive development, but we do not fully understand why some of us turn out one way and others quite different. Despite the complexities, let us take a deep breath and plunge into this fascinating world – logos, the mind, and its mysterious machinations.

WHAT IS THE MIND?

In his book *The Mindful Therapist: A Clinician's Guide to Mindsight and Neural Integration*, Dr. Daniel J. Siegel writes that the vast majority of mental health professionals have not yet developed a definition of the mind. Of the 85,000 therapists across four continents, fewer than 5% have had even one lecture defining the mind. Must not be easy, I guess.

In the book *Descartes' Error: Emotion, Reason, and the Human Brain*, author Antonio R. Damasio writes,"having a mind means that an organism forms neural representations that can become images, be manipulated in a process called thought, and eventually influence behavior by helping predict the future, plan accordingly, and choose the next action."

Quite simply, our eyes, ears – our senses of sight, sound, touch, taste, and smell – become inputs to our minds. And our images, thoughts, and behavioral reactions – emotional, intellectual, and physical – are the outputs. But no two people look at the same situation and react precisely the same way, nor do they have entirely identical inner experiences. Based on our experiences and beliefs, a veggie burger is a hearty meal for one, but an epic disappointment for a meat lover. Each of us processes these inputs and outputs differently, based on a vast number of possibilities.

The basics of our mind are pretty much the same for most of us. We have emotions, desires, and we make a mish-mash of these to make decisions. And then there are nuances for each, making each of us somewhat special, kinda crazy in our own way. Some have a stronger emotional filter and others are more logical. These impact our behaviors and decisions. But rule number one is that we are all crazy. We are all broken. And we are all striving all the time to fill those holes inside our psyche.

All that I see, hear, taste, smell, and touch are the creations of my mind.

– Nikos Kazantzakis, The Saviors of God

Inside Bill's Brain

Interviewer: Your brain is a CPU?

Bill Gates: Yes.

Interviewer: What is your worst fear?

Bill Gates: Mmm . . . I don't want my brain to stop working.

Source: From the Netflix series Inside Bill's Brain.

Figure 11-2 **The mind as a CPU – inputs and outputs.**

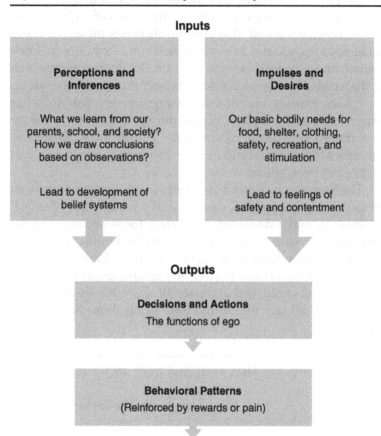

Inputs

Perceptions and Inferences

What we learn from our parents, school, and society? How we draw conclusions based on observations?

Lead to development of belief systems

Impulses and Desires

Our basic bodily needs for food, shelter, clothing, safety, recreation, and stimulation

Lead to feelings of safety and contentment

Outputs

Decisions and Actions
The functions of ego

Behavioral Patterns
(Reinforced by rewards or pain)

Putting It in Computer Jargon

Geeks and technology nerds will draw analogies of the mind to the central processing unit (CPU) – a chip inside every computer that does all the logical heavy lifting in conjunction with the software layers that govern the CPU's operations (see Figure 11.2). The mind is more like the operating system (OS) – the software that runs silently, like a conductor of a symphony making no music yet everything depends on the wave of its baton, ensuring that all parts work together, harmoniously, efficiently, elegantly, to create a powerful experience.

Computer scientist extraordinaire Alan Turing once argued that "my mind as I know it cannot be compared to a machine." That is certainly true. Our minds are far more than a sterile input-output machine. But for the purposes of our journey, let us simplify it as a simple machine. In goes bread and wine, out comes a sigh or peals of laughter (which might depend on the quality of the wine).

Toward Pleasure and Away from Pain

Just as the mind pushes us to fulfill our desires, seek pleasure and satisfaction, it also helps us run away from ambiguity and discomfort. When in pain, we find the wave swell of fear, anxiety, anger, envy, aversion, resentment . . . And then we hit escape, to gravitate toward safety, comfort, and certainty.

This pattern plays out in the world of business and start-ups as well. Notice how, when we have a cash flow crisis, or our competition makes threatening moves, or another company raises a ton of capital – our restlessness and agitation escalates. We feel unsafe, trapped by our financial maze of debt, flailing revenue projections, down rounds, and falling stock prices.

It's not just an individual who struggles with certainty; the entire financial system – Wall Street – rewards certainty. Whether it is quarterly earnings or revenue growth, predictability is a good thing. Any earnings disappointment is met with a severe punishment – an instant price drop of the stock. Six consecutive quarters of market earnings disappointment and the CEO is out. The vast majority of our society is driven by these two forces: pulled toward pleasure and repelled from pain.

THE THREE BROAD FUNCTIONS OF OUR MIND

If we were to list the three core functions of our mind, it would quite simply consist of our ability to be present, to make decisions, and to use our memory for our greater good. A well-oiled machine performs its primary tasks well and when we

find ourselves bogged down under overwhelming circumstances, these three areas often start to show some chinks in
our cognitive armor.

1. **Attention and Concentration** refer to our ability to stay
   focused on a conversation, a book we might be reading, a
   task, or an event. It's a curious blend of awareness, focus,
   and being engaged. This fundamental ability to take in
   the stimuli around us and process it quickly defines our
   productivity. Imagine a neurosurgeon or an airline pilot
   with poor concentration, perpetually distracted flitting
   from one random thought to another. For most of us,
   sustained concentration is much harder in the day and
   age of 45 open browser tabs, machine-generated alerts,
   notifications, likes, and tweets. The apps and alerts trying to get and lock our attention into perpetuity feed us
   targeted ads and show our cognitive abilities no kindness. As our minds scatter the hours away in Doom
   scrolling, we also lose one of our fundamental strengths.

---

*I have a room, which is in my brain, and it's very, very,
very . . . untidy! There is stuff fallen everywhere. There are some
very important ideas next to some very silly ones. There is a bottle
of wine that was opened five years ago, and there is a lunch I
haven't eaten from last summer. There are faces of children who are
going to die but don't have to. There's my father's face telling me
to tidy up my room. So that's what I'm doing – tidying my room.*
   *– Singer and Songwriter of U2, Bono, in conversation
      with Michka Assaya*

---

2. **Analyze and Discriminate** – This is how we pick a path,
   choose, decide, and make a call. How do we lift up the
   scale of pros and cons, weigh the proverbial scales, be a
   critic, or a judge? Our analytical abilities not only help
   us to stay safe and run away from a wild boar that might
   attack us, on a better day, it also helps us make the right
   turn on the street and rapidly sift through the myriad
   options while ordering a venti-latte at a Starbucks.

- Inductive – a set of observations, leads to identification of patterns and development of theory.

- Deductive – build a hypothesis, collect data, and test them, analyze results, if data supports the thesis, proved. If data does not support the thesis, too bad. Start all over again.

Our mind shifts into a different gear when morality comes into play. I'll say more of this in the following chapters, but the analytical engine gets stuck – even goes wonky – the moment our beliefs start to impinge on its functioning.

3. **Memory, Retention, and Recall** – Our minds determine what to store, retain, and recall. All the tiny bits of information, flashbulb events, moments ecstatic and traumatic are all stored away. Memory is closely tied to the first two functions – concentration and discrimination.

   Memory can be our friends or our enemies, depending on how it serves us. When it serves us well, we use our memory for progress and service. Memory becomes our enemy when we brood over past traumatic experiences and we get caught in the groove of rumination. Although we think of our memory as one big blob floating somewhere in our cranium, experts believe that we have as many as five types of memory systems.

   - *Working Memory – used for short-term tasks*
   - *Episodic Memory – personally experienced events, meaningful events in life*
   - *Semantic Memory – where we store facts, data, vocabulary for spelling bees and such*
   - *Procedural Memory – where we retain various routines and skills, such as riding bicycles, flying a kite, or swimming*
   - *Perceptual Representation – in which abstract connections reside often outside of our conscious awareness (example – racial bias)*

Memory – Building a Start-up Narrative

We remember the joy and pain: our summer vacation in the halcyon childhood days, our first kiss etched in our hearts, or the self-confidence rush that came with our first paycheck. All these events get cached away and often come rushing back at other times. We transcend time and space, back into those cocoons of wonderful feelings – love, warmth, joy, and bliss. We often try to recreate these feelings many times over – an addiction to that dopamine rush. On the flip side, in this vast storehouse of memory, we also stuff and hoard painful traumatic events of the past, its fear, and terror. Memory does not discriminate. It takes everything as it comes. We bury these dark traumatic memories away and try to avoid resurfacing them at all costs. But these show up in our actions or patterns. Where exactly we store these memories is a mystery as well. Some agree that parts of our brain cells are the storage chambers. Other theories include the whole cellular body to be a memory-library of sorts. It really doesn't matter where it's stored. As long as it functions well and serves us to meet our needs.

. . . he'll read 14 books while on vacation and reads 150 pages an hour . . . that's a gift. I'm gonna say it's 90 percent retention. Kind of extraordinary.

– Speaking about Bill Gates
(from Inside Bill's Brain, Netflix series)

Studies show that our memory can be tricky, selective, adapting, and not completely reliable. We can choose to remember some events and bury others completely. At times, we may be unable to recall names, historic events, and information when needed. Others can go on to win all sorts of memory championships. And, we even conjure up events that may have never occurred.

In several studies of memory recall, researchers have found that our memory of major events is not fixed. It evolves as time passes, as we forget some parts while we add other parts (that may have never occurred). "Memory's truth, because memory has its own special kind. It selects, eliminates, alters, exaggerates, minimizes, glorifies, and vilifies also; but in the end it creates its own reality, its heterogeneous but usually coherent version of events; and no sane human being ever trusts someone else's version more than his own," writes Salman Rushdie in his Booker Prize–winning work of fiction, *Midnight's Children*. One researcher describes our memory to be somewhat like that of a Wikipedia page: it can be altered and deleted as our narrative changes, and others even contribute to the narrative, quite generously. We just don't know when these subtle introductions occur, nor do we include footnotes or references. It's a constantly evolving fluidic moss-pit. Memory is not like a hard drive where we file away memories and then retrieve them with a simple double-click of the brain-mouse. Memory is an active, reconstructive process. Our memories are based around the gist of information. We often drop details without realizing it and then end up inferring them (aka making them up) when we reconstruct the memory, later on, writes Melanie Tannenbaum in *The Scientific American*. In his book, *Forgetting: Myths, Perils and Compensations*, author Douwe Draaisma describes a curious case of imaginary memories, where volunteers believed something that had never occurred; even added fantastic imaginary details.

I find this to be true when we ask a founder about their original inspiration – why did they start the company? Unfortunately, the narrative nonsense is full of made up stuff. Storytelling arcs scripted by coaches and sprinkled with inspirational incense, doled with gobs of self-belief and false passion. The audience no longer believes in such theatrical moves. Many investors have flat out stopped asking questions of this kind, which generate such nonsense.

Putting it all together, our mind has inputs and outputs. The sensory inputs bring in all kinds of external data and images. And, our mind analyzes, processes, and develops our thoughts, words, and actions as outputs. To process the inputs and generate outputs, our faculties of focus, reason, and memory come into play. And, that's more or less how the average human mind functions. Our minds use their core functions of attention, concentration, memory, recall, and analysis to perform some "executive functions" that come into effect in our daily work routines. These are:

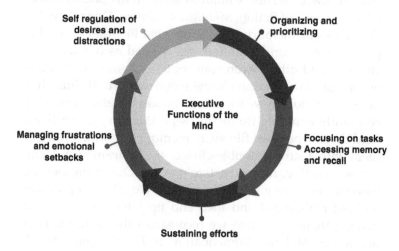

When stress and anxiety take over, many of these executive functions of our mind go numb. Some, even all, become dysfunctional.

"Executive dysfunction" is getting really common in young people because we're so saturated with multitasking and interruption that it's shortening our attention spans. And in my case, I was trying to hold these huge problem spaces in my head. So my motivation was completely exhausted day in and day out, and I couldn't even manage to do something as minor as getting a letter in the mail . . . I'd put it off for weeks

– from hackernews

And with all this cognitive overload, founders do not get time out. The engine keeps running and we are expected to make a hundred important decisions each day. This interplay of information overload, speed of decision-making, limited resources, and our idealistic belief systems can fracture our minds. We can barely prioritize (feeling overwhelmed) nor focus on tasks for longer than three minutes or sustain efforts in any meaningful way. Our frustrations overrun us and trigger anger, anxiety, or sadness. And our memory often becomes our own enemy, regurgitating all the traumatic experiences we have endured. Our self-regulation pretty much falls apart, our desires take over, and we take solace in any substance that can bring us some relief. Whiskey, anyone?

The Founder's Mind

The mind of a founder works somewhat differently from most. It seeks and chooses risk to fill some unknown void in its psyche. Choosing risk is a behavior that cannot be categorized as something that comes from a rational mind. A founder ignores a wide range of screaming "are you crazy to attempt this?" signals and selects a few perspectives that confirm their own worldviews. The mind of a founder refuses to get bogged down by the immensity of problems. This is its immense strength, as well as its greatest weakness. Because a founder has been encouraged to "never never never never give up" or to "keep fighting" with all the inspirational memes, they do not know when to stop or to pause for rest and recovery. They do not know how to ask for help when they are wounded or overwhelmed. They behave as if they are invincible, unbreakable.

To understand that weakness, failing, and shortcoming, we have to look at our own minds from another objective vantage point. We don't quite know how to self-assess. Often we end up staring at our glorious image in a mental mirror and succumb to self-praise. The Dunning-Kruger effect, where we overestimate our abilities compared to our actual skills, plays out each time. So we often fool ourselves and don't even know it. Indeed this is one of the hardest tasks that lie before us. Looking at ourselves objectively is like invoking a different part of us, maybe our third eye. The observer and the observed are the same – and yet, not the same.

A founder's self-assessments might read like the lines of the bard himself:

What a piece of work is man,
How noble in reason, how infinite in faculty,
In form and moving how express and admirable,
In action how like an Angel,
In apprehension how like a God,
The beauty of the world, The paragon of animals.

– Shakespeare, *Hamlet*, Act II, Scene 2

Founders' confidence is their ally. Their lack of self-awareness is their Achilles, heel. How does confidence build up, and how do our belief systems amplify our confidence? And what can we do about the Achilles, heel?

12

Pathos: Belief Systems

While the development of our logical thinking is occurring on one side of our heads, how do our beliefs get formed? How do these beliefs impact our logic and behavior? Do our beliefs generate an internal narrative and make our decision-making processes easier? Or do they drive up our pathos (emotion) and sufferings?

Indeed, if you start to peel the layers of belief systems, you might find that a sweeping range of beliefs – especially around the notion of God and religion are being put in practice all around – all these can be very polarizing, divisive, and can lead to bloodshed. Yet how do beliefs proliferate?

OUR BELIEFS DRIVE OUR BEHAVIORS

For some of our most important beliefs we have no evidence at all, except that people we love and trust hold these beliefs. Considering how little we know, the confidence we have in our beliefs is preposterous. . .
– Daniel Kahneman in his book Thinking, Fast and Slow

Kahneman's view is that our fast-thinking modes generate impressions, feelings, and inclinations; when endorsed by our slower side of the brain they become beliefs, attitudes, and intentions. Our foundational beliefs – whether they're formed around God, karma, the nature of people, or the presence of aliens – can drive our behavior and actions.

How do our moral beliefs get formed, and how do they influence our decision-making abilities? What helps us decide good versus bad once our belief systems jump into the mix? Our analytical abilities seem to vanish when legacy belief systems and social order comes to the forefront.

Handed down from generations, our beliefs are a smorgasbord of what parents told us, religious undertones of heaven and hell, karma, and other abstract ideas mired in social and political motivations. These beliefs often expand, forming social norms, behavioral patterns of what is accepted and what is not, and what is right and what is wrong.

Why do these beliefs get etched in our psyche and evolve at a glacial pace? Swaths of our society struggle with issues that are ingrained yet outright abhorrent. These issues stick with us, serving some dark purpose. Whether they maintain our power positions or our habitual patterns, belief systems are a double-edged sword; they represent the past trying to maintain a status quo while the future is trying to move past the relics. The social inequities against race, especially African Americans, have been a longstanding stain on our collective order. Gay rights activists fought for half a century to get legal status in America. Race, gender, slavery, and supremacy . . . the list goes on. Women get paid 70 cents to every dollar earned by men. In some countries like Russia, Saudi Arabia, and Pakistan, a woman's options might be limited when it comes to choosing her spouse, driving a car, or working as an aviation engineer.

Spanish philosopher José Ortega y Gasset wrote that beliefs constitute the base of our life, the land upon which we live. He writes, "*man, at heart, is believing . . . the deepest stratum of our life, the spirit that maintains and carries all the others, is formed by beliefs . . .*" Once we formulate our beliefs, these become invisible guardrails for most of our actions. Over time, as these behaviors become ingrained in our psyche, we often fall into an autopilot mode.

Reflections for founders and entrepreneurs might include:

- *What role did my family play in establishing my belief systems?*
- *How did the social order around me enforce or assert those beliefs?*
- *How do my belief systems help, encourage, or dampen my journey?*
- *Which belief systems no longer serve me?*
- *What new information and observations do I need to adapt my beliefs – especially the ones that do not serve me well and cause hurdles, stress, or indecision?*

OUR BELIEFS DICTATE OUR NARRATIVES

"The confidence that individuals have in their beliefs depends mostly on the quality of the story they can tell about what they see, even if they see little . . . your emotional attitude to such things as irradiated food, red meat, nuclear power, tattoos, or motorcycles drives your beliefs about their benefits and their risks," Kahneman points out.

Founders are well served if they can develop healthy belief systems – those that amplify their strengths and raise their self-image. Before starting the journey, you need ample reserves and belief systems to act as reservoirs of energy. Self-propagating, confidence-enhancing belief systems are essential to any founder's mantra. Tenacity, perseverance, and positive attitudes are behavioral outcomes that start with deeper belief systems. A sense of ambition is ingrained in our psyches, as a way to progress – to advance ourselves, our wealth and agendas, our society. But this notion of ambition is a relatively recent phenomenon, partly induced by the machines of commerce.

IS AMBITION A VICE OR VIRTUE? IT DEPENDS ON WHAT YOU BELIEVE

Prior to the sixteenth century, author David Wootton reminds us, *the desire to get ahead and do better than others was universally condemned as a vice*. In those times, innovation, industry, profits, and economic incentives were not the norm. It was in the sixteenth century that the printing press was introduced, and then on December 31,1600, Queen Elizabeth chartered the British East India Company – call it the first start-up, backed by the Queen herself. Monopolistic trade for spices, jewels, and textiles fueled a frenzy among investors and board members and helped fill the coffers of the Crown. These early developments fueled new desires and shifted our belief systems.

Today, ambition is no longer a vice; in fact, it is a virtue, a must-have in the land of entrepreneurship. Yet while we fuel ambition, we choose to not pay attention to its dark side: competition for resources. Ambition is the first step, a spark that starts the fire – but it's often courage that determines how we compete to win resources. (See Table 12.1.)

Table 12-1 **Belief Systems**

Belief Systems	Perspectives	Behaviors
Abundance/Scarcity	There are plenty of customers/opportunities, resources, and room in the market.	I operate with a sense of confidence and lightness of being.
	The customer has a limited budget. The VC has limited capital.	I operate with a sense of urgency and fear. Only the paranoid survive.
Competition	I enjoy competition, like any other game. My competition keeps me agile. It validates the market opportunity.	Let's go to war.
	Competition is unhealthy because it leads to a race to the bottom.	It's best to start companies in greenfield areas with no competition.
People	People are kind, self-motivated, and will do the right thing in any given set of circumstances.	I trust people and let them be.
	People are lazy and need to be controlled, managed, or whipped.	I try to manage every step of their workflows.

When our ambitions fail to achieve their mark, we get fatigued. Our feelings in turn chip away at our belief systems. A prolonged sense of frustration can wear down the most resilient among us.

In your darkest hour, what belief systems will you hold firm? And what belief systems will you change? Will your circumstances shape you? Or can you shape your world despite the circumstances?

In his darkest hour, while languishing for 27 years in prison, Nelson Mandela, the first president of South Africa and Nobel Peace Prize winner, found his strength in the words of William Ernest Henley:

Invictus

-William Ernest Henley

Out of the night that covers me,
Black as the pit from pole to pole,
I thank whatever gods may be
For my unconquerable soul.
In the fell clutch of circumstance
I have not winced nor cried aloud.
Under the bludgeonings of chance
My head is bloody, but unbowed.
Beyond this place of wrath and tears
Looms but the Horror of the shade,
And yet the menace of the years
Finds and shall find me unafraid.
It matters not how strait the gate,
How charged with punishments the scroll,
I am the master of my fate,
I am the captain of my soul.

13

Putting It All Together

Our desires, ego, and beliefs drive our personal growth and help manage the various transitional points in our life. In a similar manner, our organizational goals move from start-up/ survival to thriving and growth. Maslow's hierarchy of needs, a suitable analog can help us map out the phases of evolution (see Table 13.1).

First, we have to fulfill the base layer, and then we grow into the next. If the layer below is constrained or challenged, then we are unable to transition to the next level. Only when we can eat well and sleep comfortably do we feel a sense of safety, and then do our feelings of belonging arise.

A start-up's journey is somewhat similar. Once we gather some resources – say, a seed round and initial founding team – can we start building the product. As the product is ready, we start to build the business side of the organization. The financial stability of the business comes into play. Can we

Table 13-1 **Hierarchy of Needs**

Maslow's Hierarchy of Needs	Organizational Hierarchy of Needs
Achieving one's full potential/self-fulfillment	Purpose, mission, social recognition, impact, and value created
Feeling of accomplishment/self-esteem	Strategy, growth, profitability, and productivity of company
Belonging and intimacy/love	People – Team dynamics and corporate culture
Safety and security	Product – Stability and market need Operational efficiencies, daily sprints/routines
Food, clothing, shelter/basic needs	Resources – Cash/payroll, team members

Table 13-2 **Internal and External Stressors**

Internal Stressors	External Stressors
Founders unable to shift from a product mindset to a sales mindset	Customer adoption rate, next-round funding
Founders unable to shift from sales mindset to scaling and growth mindset	Competition, attraction of talent, funding
Founders unable to shift from growth mindset to building organizational culture	Retention/flight of talent due to chaos
Founders unable to shift from organizational building to competitive strategy and achieving category leadership	Shrinking profit margins, growth rates plateau
Founders unable to impact the society/community in meaningful ways	Flight of talent due to lack of purpose, sustained meaning

make payroll? Is this profitable? Is this a sustainable business? When we are starting with the basics, we are focused on survival. When we have survival figured out, we strive toward growth. We pay little attention to the higher purpose. As the start-up becomes bigger and a real company, it is subject to various external pressures and internal growth challenges (see Table 13.2). The competition starts to enter the field, team members churn, investors demand growth, urging us to keep up with every other unicorn.

As these stressors come into effect, CEO transitions often occur, as people are unable to scale as fast as the company. Amidst these step-functions, it is often the mission and the purpose that acts as a glue to hold it all together. Founders rarely focus on the mission in the formative early stages of any company because, well, we are in survival mode. So who has time for this mumbo-jumbo? We need to get the product out ASAP, attract customers, manage cash flow, and raise capital. Yet, establishing the mission is a simple starting point in building a resilient start-up. There is a reason why the term "missionary zeal" is widely prevalent in start-up circles. It keeps us going in troubled times. It does not take too long to reflect upon the mission and values. Writing these down is the easy part. Putting them in practice is much harder. The exercise is often worth the effort in the long run, because in any situational crisis, the mission can align the inner compass.

The mission and purpose act as the North Star as well as the anchor. The missionary zeal, or the superego, drives us in the long run, the skillful navigation of resources, thanks to the ego, helps us meet our performance goals, and our id makes sure our most basic needs are met.

Adam Neumann, founder and CEO of WeWork, a $47 billion company, started with a mission that resonated with investors and start-ups alike. He was unable to work his way down into the prudent financial management part of the business. The company imploded, destroying over $40 billion of value.

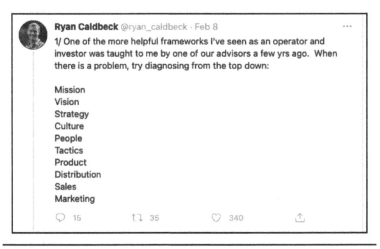

Ryan Caldbeck @ryan_caldbeck · Feb 8

1/ One of the more helpful frameworks I've seen as an operator and investor was taught to me by one of our advisors a few yrs ago. When there is a problem, try diagnosing from the top down:

Mission
Vision
Strategy
Culture
People
Tactics
Product
Distribution
Sales
Marketing

💬 15   ↻ 35   ♡ 340   ⬆

Source: Twitter, Inc.

As Ryan Caldbeck, CEO, tweeted, when there is any problem in the start-up, we should start dissecting it from the top of the pyramid and work our way down.

The mission and purpose act as the North star as well as the anchor. The mission may zeal, or the superego, drives us in their long run, the skillful navigation of resources depths to the ego, helps us meet our performance goals and our id makes sure our most basic needs are met.

Adam Neumann, founder and CEO of WeWork, a $47 billion company started with a mission that resonated with investors and start-ups alike. He was unable to work his way down into the prudent, truthful material parent part of the business. The company imploded destroying over $40 billion of value.

As Ryan Caldbeck, CEO, tweeted, when there is any problem in the start-up, we should start dissecting it from the top of the pyramid and work our way down

Part III

Reassembling the Furniture

In which we understand the role of therapy in addressing the conflicting demands of our egos, desires, and belief systems.

14

Toward Building
a Healthy Ego

Modern psychology should be just as concerned about our strengths . . . as our weaknesses. It should help build the best things in life while repairing the worst. And focus on making the lives of normal people fulfilling, nurturing high talent while relieving misery. The skills required to decrease misery and the skills required to build a positive psychology are different. With positive psychology, our life is filled with pleasure, with engagement, and with a higher purpose.

– Dr. Martin Seligman, former president of American Psychological Association, who developed tenets of positive psychology while working with "extremely miserable people"

WHAT IS A HEALTHY EGO?

Entrepreneurs do not have normal egos. If they did, they would not choose such a life riddled with risks, uncertainties, and madness. Yet what is the scale of abnormal ego? Is it a wild horse, unbridled and gone berserk, trampling others while amassing power or wealth; is it someone who is socially inept and immersed in self-absorption. Or is it a person who is mild, mellow, and soft, who might operate in self-defense, caution and protectiveness, creating a safe cocoon for herself, never being able to shake up the world.

Unfortunately, no text alert, notification, alarm bell, or "check engine" light comes on when our egos start to go out of balance. The only way to know is to do a brutally honest self-analysis.

The healthy ego diagnostic is broken down along the following four areas:

1. *Impulses and desires* – Elon Musk has a desire to inhabit the planet Mars. He also irritated the SEC with his tweets and smoked marijuana once. Others have a desire to eat chocolate cake, watch Netflix, and chill. Can we postpone, deny, or control desires, crazy aspirations, and addictions effectively? Which ones do we succumb to?

2. *Skills* – Are we able to predict outcomes of our actions? Can we tackle our day-to-day challenges? How do we prioritize our tasks and focus on what matters most? Can we silence out the unwanted noise and stimulus? On some days, I feel like a lumpy pile of Jello. I do not want to get out of bed. Can I just do the bare minimum?

3. *Self-view* – Invincible superheroes, aren't we? What do we say when we speak to our inner selves? Do we treat ourselves with a balanced view of self-respect, without inflating our egos? Is it the harsh critic, yelling all the time or a peaceful zen monk – a kind and loving parent comforting, consoling, and putting a warm blanket on our aching souls?

4. *Worldview* – How do we look at the world and the people we engage? What filters and beliefs come into play? Do we think of people as stepping stones toward meeting our selfish financial goals? Or do we see each one as a divine spirit, trying to achieve their highest potential? Do we engage with kindness and fairness, keeping everyone's interests at heart, or do we serve our own needs all the time?

Let us start with our impulses, those crazy chemical reactions inside that can hijack us, surprise us, or throw us off guard.

ARE YOU ABLE TO CONTROL YOUR IMPULSES?

Most of us are a messy pile of desires and fears. Our brains are wired to be distracted, tickled, or drawn to a number of passing distractions. Our senses – the inputs are not really helping here – the eyes, ears, nose, mouth, and skin create this complex medley of ongoing demands. One demand that we can all relate to is food and drink. On one morning, I counted the number of times I opened my mouth to snack, drink, or munch, and by 11 a.m., I had exceeded 20 times. It was mildly depressing, and I gave up counting for the rest of the day. Other desires that drive us include our daily addictions, such as caffeine. If we prevent enough people from having their daily drip of freshly brewed Sumatran coffee, we might trigger an uprising. Keep a cheesecake on the table after a hearty dinner and watch it evaporate. On a given day, keep track of the number of times we impulsively reach for the cookie jar, a sip of coffee, or some potato chips. Or even a drink of water. Most of these are harmless habitual grazing activities, but our impulse-control abilities might be limited.

In the United States, two out of three adults are overweight or obese. We cannot blame it all on the delicious food displays, baking competitions, and other similar assaults coming from the Food Channel. An ongoing stimulus-reaction dance has almost 66% of the US population struggling to control a basic stimulus – food. And we haven't even looked at various other addictions and instant-gratification tactics.

The marshmallow test – one of the famous Stanford experiments on delayed gratification showed that when children were able to exercise impulse control – to avoid eating a cookie for 15 minutes – they grew up to have better life outcomes, as measured by scholastic aptitude test (SAT) scores, educational attainment, body mass index (BMI), and ability to be resilient.

Measurements of Resilience

When it came to delaying that impulse to grab the goddamned cookie, kids developed a range of tactics. Some made up songs to distract themselves, others hid their head in their arms, pounded their feet on the floor, fiddled teasingly with the signal bell, prayed to the ceiling, and in one fascinating case – one little girl, after obviously experiencing much agitation, rested her head, relaxed, and fell asleep.

Measurements of resilience included:

- *Persistent in activities/does not give up easily*
- *Plans, thinks ahead, and responds to reason*
- *Reflective – deliberates before speaking or acting*
- *Becomes rattled or disorganized under stress*
- *Overreacts to minor frustrations, is easily irritated or angered*
- *Becomes anxious when the environment is unpredictable or poorly structured*

All impulse creates a stimulus. Can we stay patient with that impulse, pause, delay the reaction, play whack-a-mole, or even sleep over it? How do we screen out all that nonsensical stimuli, and act on only the ones that matter? The sign of a healthy ego is to be able to judiciously manage our impulses.

Too many channels and not enough emotional or intellectual support – everyone is too busy, there's no time to slow down, educate, prepare enough, feel prepared, help each other, and develop empathy. Everyone is running on flight or fight, so tempers are short. We're all just surviving. In that mode, people tend to focus on defending and protecting themselves, so teamwork falls apart.

– Start-up leader, Sydney, Australia[1]

Figure 14-1 **Moving fluidly between zones of intensity and relaxation.**

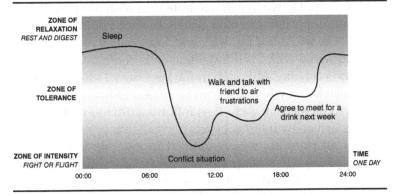

Source: J. Miller and J. Chipchase, "Emotional Resilience in Leadership Report," 2020.

Take the example of a typical day in a founder's life. It's filled with a thousand soap operas, roller coaster rides, and ups and downs. And as one founder gleefully said, "When that stuff hits the fan, it's never distributed evenly, so we run toward the places of maximum damage and try to clean it up." Being in a perpetual firefighting mode can drain our resources and have a long-term impact on our cognition. Figure 14.1 shows a typical rollercoaster of a day in the founder's life where feelings can oscillate between rest and relaxation to fight-or-flight reactions.

Skills: Are You Able to Make Judgment Calls and Predict Probable Outcomes of Your Actions?

Judgment calls are the cognitive functions of a rational mind, grounded by social and community rules. How should we act in certain circumstances and constraints? What might be the consequences of our actions? In computer jargon, think of these as a series of "if-then" statements.

If I drive above the speed limit, then I may get a speeding ticket. Of course, outcomes can vary based on the circumstances. Is it midnight? The probability of cops floating around might be lower. Is it midnight on December 31st? Well, the probability just went up. Do we live in a remote area with no traffic cops? Then we don't get speeding tickets but we could hit a wild animal. Or, while texting, we could lose control of the car and hurtle down a cliff. Such judgment calls come into play each hour and each day. Although traffic laws, social safety rules are pretty black and white, a lot can be subject to interpretation. In our own microcosm, each of us follows a different internal set of rules driven by internal beliefs and existing priorities.

Not all rules are crisply defined in neat black and white squares. Subjective interpretations infuse any situation. Moral dilemmas create variants in our behavior. We know we should not text and drive, but when a loved one texts us, we succumb to temptation. Or for example, if we cheat someone, a guilty conscience – the superego – storms into the scene. Our actions also have social repercussions, and if we violate norms, we damage our credibility and reputation or face legal liabilities. Religious and social belief systems often factor into this equation. Judgment calls are never easy. Situations are never quite crisp or black and white. During such times, how do we make judgment calls? A healthy ego never misses a beat. It scans the situation and makes a swift move.

Self-view: Are You Able to Adjust Your Views When Situations Change?

Do extraneous events trigger a sense of helplessness? The world around us is changing, not exactly the way we want and sometimes too fast. At the macro level, we have pandemics, stock market gyrations, social unrest, and tyrannical and despotic presidents. At the company level, we are busy managing cash flows, team members, politics, valuations, and growth rates – the business keeps changing and evolving. Can we deal with all of these rapid events? Some find it unsettling and can't keep up. Others do it with panache.

Often when situations around us change, we run away (flight) or we enter into a combat (fight) to defeat the situation.

However, in some situations, we can neither fight nor run away. Take the pandemic, for example, during which most of us were trapped into our Zoom boxes, unable to do what we were used to. Some CEOs I talked to had an innate sense of new opportunities that were arising. Others were resigned to the fact that it was "game over." Some moved – away from cities into other (tax friendly) cities like Austin or Miami, whereas some went to the ski-friendly zones like Bozeman, Montana, or even Singapore. Each adapted in his or her own way, staying frozen or helpless.

An agile ego can help us adapt to the situation around us and help us stay on course. Adaptation is essential, and I could quote Darwin's much amplified quote on survival of the ones who could adapt. It is a life-saving skill indeed. Adaptation is easier said than done but we often fail to ask why we are fighting external situations. Those who refuse to adapt often end up in a lonely, muddy, and a compromised state. In resisting change, we might try various tactics – we push, we pull, we scream, we curl up in a ball and cry, or we retreat. When we do not get what we want from life, we seek an escape hatch. We take our toys and run away from the playground to find some place of solace. In our retreat, withdrawn and alone, we become like wounded animals that hide in the forest to heal. We seek meditation retreats in Nepal, pilgrimages in Rome, or a trip to Israel. We seek some solace. Amidst all this churning, we reflect, learn, and come to terms with external realities.

Some of us can remain trapped in childlike innocent states and leave us hopelessly unprepared for some challenges that come about in our lives. Our fantasies, secret rings, magic wands, castles, and superheroes continue to play out in our adulthood. Our expectations of achieving immortality, fame, fortune, and glory do not pan out quite the way we had imagined when our life imagined and life reality collide. As the lines from "Paranoid Eyes," a song by Pink Floyd go, "You believed in their stories of fame, fortune glory. Now you're lost in a haze of alcohol soft middle age. The pie in the sky turned out to be miles too high . . ."

Adapting a new perspective when your house burns down. . . .

When Thomas Edison lost most of his work to a raging fire, Edison told his 24-year-old son, Charles, "Go get your mother and all her friends. They'll never see a fire like this again." Several buildings were ablaze as the firefighters tried their best to put it out. When Charles objected, Edison said, "It's all right. We've just got rid of a lot of rubbish." Later, he said, "Although I am over 67 years old, I'll start all over again tomorrow." He began rebuilding the next morning without firing any of his employees.

World View: How Do You See the World Around You?

Whereas self-view is going inward, and creating an image of ourselves, the worldview is everything out there and how we perceive it. Do we see the world as a jungle, where animals are out to eat each other after dark, or is it largely a community of do-gooders, each trying to help the other? Do we see abundance or do we see scarcity of resources? Do you see people as largely lazy, selfish beings or are they self-governing responsible and effective members of the society? Do you see the world as a magical grain of sand in this huge cosmos as God's work or do you see it as a chaotic system spinning toward entropy and disorder?

Our worldview defines some of our behavioral dynamics and rules of engagement. For founders, a view of scarcity often drives them to behave in one way, while those who operate with a sense of abundance move at a different pace, marching to a different drumbeat.

HOW DOES YOUR EGO PROTECT YOU WHEN YOU FEEL UNSAFE?

As we engage with the world, we often find ourselves in stressful situations. We might resort to fight or flight – offensive mode or defensive retreat. Our strength depends on the context and the perceived strength of our opponent. In such situations, four levels of defense mechanisms operate within our ego's repertoire. See Figure 14.2.

Figure 14-2 **Four defense mechanisms.**

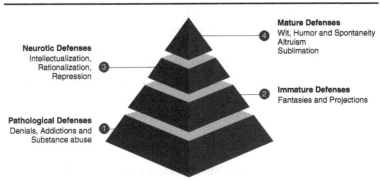

Psychiatrist and Harvard Medical School professor George Vaillant has studied human behavior for 30 years and introduced a four-level classification of our defense mechanisms. These mechanisms often occur in subtle autopilot ways. We often do not realize when such behavior kicks in. But all these save us and help reduce our anxiety around stressful situations.

Level I – Pathological Defenses

Denial of behaviors: We are unaware of our addictive patterns of behavior – alcohol, workahol – and we become so consumed that not only do we fail to recognize our addictions, we would vehemently deny those patterns if someone were to stick a mirror in our face and point those out to us.

Level II – Immature Defenses

Fantasy: Ask anyone who has suffered from pangs of unrequited love and unfulfilled relationships and we will see their world of fantasies, thanks to their indulgence in romantic fairy tales, white picket fences, and palatial homes by the lake in utopian lands of perfectly happy singsong lives that do not exist. Other forms of fantasy include self-proclaimed emperorship of America.

Projection: As is our emotional state, so is our view of the world. Or, as they say, as inside, so outside. We see our disowned and unacceptable qualities in other people. For example, if we have a strong dislike for someone, we might instead believe that they do not like us. Passive-aggressive behavior/acting out – we indirectly express our anger or dissatisfaction in a number ways, including stalling, avoidance, and more. This is a classic Level II immature defense.

Fantasy: San Francisco Entrepreneur Anoints Himself as Emperor of America

When Joshua Abraham Norton first arrived in San Francisco in the eighteenth century, he made a comfortable living as a commodities trader and real estate baron. However, he soon lost it all, became bankrupt and broke, and disappeared for several years. He made a grand reappearance introducing himself as Emperor of these United States, at the "request and desire of a large majority of these United States." The proclamation was published in San Francisco's Daily Evening Bulletin newspaper. For two decades, he "ruled" San Francisco and printed his own treasury bonds that were backed by no guarantee – much like Bitcoins of the eighteenth century. Dining establishments citywide started to accept these bonds and soon, Norton was a beloved figure. He took his emperorship quite seriously, appearing at public hearings to argue for equality; proposing ideas that were quite progressive at the time, including standing up for African Americans, fighting anti-Chinese sentiments, and defending Native Americans and women. He was the first to propose the idea of constructing a bridge that would eventually become the Golden Gate Bridge. And all of this started with a delusional Level II defense of a bankrupt commodity trader.

Level III – Neurotic Defenses

Intellectualization: We reduce our anxiety by looking at the facts and logic, staying busy analyzing everything in a cold, sterile manner. We escape and run away from our emotional sides, because these may be too heavy to bear. For example, at a funeral we stay busy making the arrangements because we do not want to deal with the process of grieving.

Rationalization: We take our unacceptable behaviors and wrap them in a rational or logical veneer, avoiding the true subconscious reasons for the behavior. And when we win, we attribute our achievements to our qualities and skills, whereas we often blame failures on others or outside forces. For example, when investors turn down founders, the founders might rationalize by saying the investor was not a good fit anyway.

Reaction formation: We become excessively friendly with those we may dislike in order to hide our true feelings. According to Freud, reaction formation is a defense mechanism to hide our true feelings by behaving in the exact opposite manner. Bizarre but true.

Disassociation: When we get lost in a book or a movie we disassociate ourselves from our surroundings. When under extremely challenging circumstances we disassociate ourselves from that pain and may have no memory of such traumatic events.

When one wants to rid oneself of an intolerable pressure, one needs hashish. Well, I needed Wagner.

– Nietzsche

Displacement: We have bad days at work when we go home to yell at our spouses or kick our dogs. We vent our frustrations at those who are weak and are unable to fight back. Subtly we know our behavior has no consequences. Displacement occurs when we subconsciously know we can get away with bad behavior, so we gladly proceed to do so.

Repression: Repressed memories of abuse manifest as difficulty in forming trusting relationships. Sometimes, we can suppress painful memories consciously by forcing unwanted information out of our awareness. In other cases, anxiety-provoking memories are unconsciously suppressed. Speaking of repression:

> *The patient does not remember what is repressed but acts it out. He reproduces it not as a memory, but as an action – he repeats it without knowing he is repeating it.*
>
> *– Sigmund Freud*

Level IV – Mature Defenses

Wit, humor, and spontaneity: We make fun of the complex situation or laugh away the anxiety.

Source: Twitter, Inc.

Sublimation: We indulge in extreme sports, buy boxing gloves and a punching bag to alleviate our aggression and release our inner frustrations.

Altruism: We try to act benevolently, aspire to see the greater good, and deviate from our anxiety-ridden situations. When we are threatened physically, our primal side kicks in, as it tries to protect, serve, and inflate itself, and we might resort to a fistfight. If the perpetrator is a 300-pound imposing hulk, we flee, run away as fast as we can to save face, and avoid a bloody nose and the trauma.

When we encounter day-to-day challenges or intellectual jujitsu, our egos will often kick in and try to protect our stance, reputation, image, and social standing. Our ego will try to protect us from shame, embarrassment, and weakness. In doing so, we try to prove we are right, smart, or cool. Sigmund Freud originally proposed that such defense mechanisms safeguard the mind against conflicts. Such conflicts may generate feelings and thoughts that are too difficult for our minds to cope with. Soon, defense mechanisms kick in. Whenever we feel threatened, we resort to these four levels of defenses – pathological, neurotic, immature, and mature.

Our goal should be to graduate to Level IV defenses. But the ultimate aim is to achieve a sense of ego mastery.

MichaelMeirSaltzman
@JustAddSaltz

I'm 35 and have not yet received a call to adventure and am starting to worry I'm not a protagonist

Source: Twitter, Inc.

CAN YOU MASTER YOUR EGO?

The pinnacle of all these ego states, termed as mastery, is when we are able to make good decisions, build strong relationships, stay anchored in reality, and tune into our circumstances so that we are functioning well, each day, and every day. A masterful ego can navigate the demands of our desires, the moral dilemmas presented by the superego, and the uncertainties life throws at you. With a strong ego, the inner landscape is resilient and competent most of the time. At the same time, we continue to be self-aware of our developmental tasks, and can give and receive appropriate feedback from our intimate relationships. Such an ego is neither inflated or oppressive, but finely balanced.

Make your ego porous. Will is of little importance, complaining is nothing, fame is nothing. Openness, patience, receptivity, solitude is everything.

– Rainer Maria Rilke

The way we experience and deal with the world, in short, is like that of a steady horse rider; not much can topple such a person. In the face of a rough wind, sandstorm, or a sirocco, the one with a masterful ego remains adept and rides along smoothly.

To recap, as we start to build a healthy ego, here are the questions we need to reflect on:

- *Are you able to control your desires and impulses?*
- *Are you able to predict outcomes of your actions?*
- *Are you able to adjust your views when external situations change?*
- *How does your ego protect you when you feel threatened?*
- *Can you master your ego so that it can deftly navigate between the constraints of your belief systems and demands of your desires?*

Building a healthy ego might require some help, just as you might get a trainer when you head to the gym. Asking for help from a counselor, therapist, guru, or shrink might be an option.

15

Psychotherapy: An Imperfect History of an Impossible Profession

The difference between neurotics and normal people is a matter only of degree. . .

– Sigmund Freud

What is therapy, and how does it exactly work? Is it a science – predictable and measurable – or an art form – blending some proven techniques with situational context. In the Western world, psychotherapy is accepted widely while in some parts of the world, our neuroticism could be addressed with traditional rituals. Like most complexities in life, the best answer will seem unsatisfactory to the fierce intellect and barely acceptable to the aching heart. We don't fully understand how our insides work, but we can make some intelligent guesses.

SIGMUND FREUD: THE PAST CREATES THE FUTURE

The father of psychotherapy Sigmund Freud was a complex personality. He liked to smoke cigars, enjoy cocaine, and even recommended it generously as an antidepressant. A prolific writer, he authored a 24-volume magnum opus of his psychological works. Although the usage of cocaine as an antidepressant can be debated, some of his writings are considered to be foundational. He constructed a range of possibilities for what caused mental health challenges. Not much was grounded in any statistical or scientific analysis. Indeed, it is not easy to develop mathematical models of such subjective processes. All that goes on in our mind is often somewhat mysterious and cannot be measured in a laboratory as yet.

Although the laws of physics and mathematics seldom change, it's both daunting as well as somewhat of a relief that the rules of psychoanalysis keep changing all the time. For one, we are not big fans of electroconvulsive therapy or cocaine; Ayahuasca maybe, but definitely not cocaine. These past artefacts of treatment are no longer seen as effective or viable.

Freud proposed that our psyche and its three parts – id, ego, and superego – help us understand that we are an incredibly complex bundle of instinctual desires, judgments, and moral values that have been infused upon us. These three parts of us are in a perpetual dance, trying to trade different pieces in our life's game. "The ego has three tyrannical masters – the id, the superego and the external world – and tries to keep harmony between these three forces," he writes. These forces have incompatible and divergent claims that cannot be satisfied simultaneously, leading to the breakdown of the ego. Just as CEOs juggling with three powers that influence them – the board of directors, their team, and the market forces – when these three have divergent and incompatible claims on CEOs' mindshares, naturally the CEOs will throw their arms up in the air. Freud's fundamental proposition is that *all psychoanalytic work is aimed at strengthening the ego*, and making it independent of the superego. Next time you read some blabbering about ego being the enemy, invoke the spirit of Freud.

Freud's theories hinged on major events in our childhood and parental care (or lack thereof), which define our deepest behavioral patterns and quirks. He postulated that our idiosyncrasies play out for the rest of our lives, and at times we are not even aware of our cyclical patterns. This also led to a somewhat unfortunate yet convenient position that we should blame our parents for everything that is wrong with us. As our past cannot be changed, we are allowed to stay grumpy and seek therapy for the rest of our lives. Childhood trauma and abuse does create major personality challenges, which could emanate for the rest of our lives. But if your little sister sneezed over your cupcake and, 20 years later, you are still traumatized by such an event, that is another matter.

In Sigmund Freud's inner circle was a Swiss psychologist called Carl Jung. Their love for the subject of human psychology was so immense that in their first meeting, their 20-year age gap notwithstanding, Freud and Carl Gustave Jung talked for 13 hours straight. Freud would go on to mentor Jung and supported his ascension to the first presidency of the International Association of Psychoanalysts. Over time, Jung expanded the foundation laid by Freud, and over time, other schools of thought sprung up.

CARL JUNG: A LOOK AT THE DARK SIDE

Jung and Freud – the two were brilliant in their own realms, yet sparks would often fly, miring their friendship in undercurrents of competitive views. They eventually fell apart, battling for dominance on *my ideas versus yours* – including theories, models, and structures of our mind, ego, and consciousness.

Jung did not believe that we were born as a clean slate, a whiteboard with no impressions. Rather, he believed there existed a collective unconscious force. His work delved into the formation of individual personas, the unknown, and the invisible side. He developed theories of our dark side or the shadow self, where our repressed side operates silently. This was extended further to our dreams, where our subconscious parts are trying to vaguely communicate our wishes and needs.

Spiritualism and mystical experiences were a part of his worldview, and when asked about God, Jung once said, "I do not need to believe in God. I know." In fact, he firmly believed that we were tied to a collective unconscious, which was like the light waves of a spectrum that are not entirely visible to the human eye. He proposed that we come into the world with inbuilt structures – preprogrammed bits of code, which he termed as archetypes. For example, he saw the archetype of Loki as a fun-loving trickster or the wise old man. Hero archetypes are woven into our daily lives – the entrepreneur, the movie star, the characters of Star Wars, or the heroes of *Lord of the Rings*. Jung's work further led to the development of assessing personalities based on a mix of intellect, emotion, and feelings – what is popularly called today the Myers-Briggs Type Indicator (MBTI).

ALFRED ADLER: THE PAST DOES NOT MATTER, JUST FOCUS ON THE PRESENT

Right around the same time as Jung was ascending to fame and psychoanalysis was gaining momentum, another Viennese doctor, Alfred Adler, was at work. Like Jung, he too was a part of Sigmund Freud's inner circle, thriving on weekly group debates while sipping black coffee, smoking cigars, and nibbling on cake. But Adler and Freud too would have a falling-out, going about their separate ways. It's funny how most of these doyens of psychology, who studied the mind and ego and stressed the importance of interpersonal relationships would themselves not be able to get along within their little group.

Alfred Adler's views were built not on the past mishaps or childhood or parental deficiencies or shortcoming, but on just focusing on the present situation. His model of therapy was built on the present goals and not much of the past. Let us try and solve our present problems and not feel utterly helpless, dwelling into our childhood, which was water beneath the proverbial bridge, beyond our control. Adler's style was pragmatic, and he wrote for the common man, avoiding big words, exotic concepts, and fancy jargon. His contributions were widely adopted without giving much credit to him. Never assuming a superior stance, he placed importance on establishing a respectful and cooperative relationship of equals with all who came to him. He cast the symbolic shrink's couch aside, making way for two chairs instead. An idealist, he aimed to democratize the field and believed that everyone in our society – parents, plumbers, teachers, and social workers, even those with no formal education, should understand basic elements of individual psychology. That way, our children would be able to wield the faculties of reason and emotion well, growing up to be balanced human beings. His holistic views were clearly ahead of his time – encompassing mind, body, and spirit, and advocating for social equality and justice. He encouraged peer therapists to view people as a whole and understand them contextually – their family, social, and cultural contexts – and bring emphasis on optimism, encouragement, empowerment, advocacy, and support. Experts bemoan that much has been borrowed from Adler's work without acknowledgment. The art of Socratic questioning and the popular Abraham Maslow's hierarchy of needs pyramid have stemmed from "The Adlerian School" of philosophical thought.

Although therapeutic techniques are too numerous, the early works of Freud, Jung, and Alfred Adler can be seen as foundational elements. Most therapeutic approaches eventually branch off from here, using parts from each. For example, we might have repressed memories of an abusive incident during our childhood (Freud) leading to a pattern of subconscious triggers and behaviors. Knowing and accepting our dark side and shadow self (Jung) helps us observe and understand our own feelings of envy, anger, emptiness, or alienation. Starting off with the challenges of the present moment (Adler) – our work and relationship challenges – the therapist might approach a problem-solution orientation.

Over 100 years ago, these fundamental techniques started to shape the foundations of therapeutic and analytical techniques.

Today, 100 different techniques are currently in practice.

Which one will work best for us?

Well, it depends – but try we must.

16

Fearing Our Own Selves . . . and Other Mental Blocks

My analysis gave me self-awareness, led me not to fear being myself.

— *Psychologist Erik H. Erikson*

Why do we fear being ourselves? Why do we lack self-awareness? How did therapy help ignite Erikson's courage to not to fear being himself? Anna Freud, Sigmund Freud's daughter, charged a princely subscription of $7 per month and met Erik Erikson almost everyday. He went on to become a renowned therapist, proposed groundbreaking theories for child development and the art of managing "identity crisis." For his writings, Erikson won the Pulitzer Prize. How did therapy lead to his self-awareness?

A therapist works to identify and activate the healing forces that exist within the patient. This process in which the two people work in tandem to ignite the forces within one is part mystical and magical and part structural, and it keeps evolving with time and culture. Take the example of Japanese therapy, which defines the *sunao mind* (which roughly translates to straightforward or uncluttered). With a *sunao* mind people would be able to endure their anxiety and dissatisfaction. Accepting oneself means admitting one's weaknesses, demerits, discomforts, and undesirable feelings as they are. With a *sunao* mind, people aspire to achieve the impossible, while establishing harmony and peace. With a start-up, founders try to achieve the impossible while running the risk of madness.

Therapy is not easy, nor it is for everyone. It is most certainly not a feel-good session, although some sessions may feel good. Not all of us have the courage to talk to a professional – as we might fear the outcomes. I would curl up and hide under a blanket if anyone were to try and dissect my inner workings and stick a mirror in my face; show me my madness, warts and all; and then go on to remove those. It is not a fun process. But by gosh, it can be rewarding, and it can be a relief.

HOW WE RESIST OUR DEVELOPMENT – IGNORANCE AND DENIAL

Founders will often subtly resist therapy, and ignore or deny all the blaring signs and signals that stare them in their faces. A founder writes, "I have bar friends – therapy is just a glorified form of a paid friendship. Some mumbo-jumbo free-flowing talk? And isn't it horrendously expensive, like $250 per hour? Good for the therapists to just sit, nod and pretend to listen, and collect a fat fee. Even that supposed one hour is short-changed to 50 minutes? How do I even know this works?"

> **Keshav**
> @narulakeshav   ...
>
> To all the founders out there:
>
> PLEASE DO NOT DE-PRIORITIZE
> YOUR MENTAL HEALTH.
>
> Over the last few months, I've
> experienced chronic stress that has
> led to my physical turmoil 😩
> Please take time off, FaceTime your
> friends, get a therapist b/c stress can
> literally kill you! 🙏
>
> 3:40 PM · 2/1/21 · Twitter Web App
>
> **15** Retweets **3** Quote Tweets **199** Likes

Source: Twitter, Inc.

Sure, you can quickly dismiss therapy and take the easy way out. That inner voice might say that therapy is just talking, right? I can call up my friend and talk to them and feel good. Or it's safer to talk to strangers in a bar. They don't know you. Some have empathy. Others might comfort us, drunk on their own pina coladas and problems. But they may be neither vested in our success nor skilled, tactful, or persistent to dig out the patterns of our behaviors. Nor would they be available at times when you need them. In such conversations, we might keep spinning around with short-term dopamine-rush fixes. In most of our relationships, we project different sides of our glorious selves to those around us. Depending on what we seek to gain, (or what we might lose in such a relationship), we may choose to be nice or be cold. Rarely are we fully authentic and transparent in our emotional states, our dark side, our fears, and our own shortcomings. Conversations with friends require a sacred pact, deep trust, and confidentiality. Will you hurt me? Or misuse my vulnerabilities to their advantage? Although friends might be good listeners, it is unlikely that friends will help us identify and skillfully tackle our inner demons or, for that matter, support us in tactical ways when we fall into patterns of negative behavior.

Another excuse we come up with is lacking resources – no time or money. We are so busy building our companies, we have important product releases/funding rounds – who has time for this? Amidst all this, how can I find a good therapist? Some of the legitimate reasons might be lack of money or health care benefits. Yet other challenges may be efficient access to trained professionals. One founder told me that he was worried about doctor-patient confidentiality, and even went as far as saying that if their medical records were compromised, hackers would shame him. He felt he had a lot more to lose than gain in seeking help.

It's okay if you don't know how exactly therapy works. But more important is the fact that you are not trapped in a world of excuses, unwilling or unable to press the eject button and take that first step toward asking for help. No more burying that leaden head in sand, you have decided to find a solution to your situation. Making an active choice to solve your own problem – for which no one knows the right solution – is a bold step, not for the faint of heart.

DISMANTLING THE BLOCKS

CEO coach, author, and former venture capital investor Jerry Colonna has committed to therapy for the rest of his life.

Why, you might ask? Working with a trained professional offers a reliable, confidential, and skillful pathway toward stability and productivity. No therapist offers a magic wand, nor can they make you "happy." Seeking happiness is not a goal. It is indeed our responsibility to make the choices that will lead us to a more balanced, productive state of mind. But a therapist, like a coach, can identify some of the stumbling blocks, and help dismantle those, one piece at a time.

Therapist and author Dr. Irvin Yalom writes, "I do not inspire the patient with desire to grow, to curiosity, will, zest for life, caring, loyalty or any of the myriad characteristics that make us fully human. No. What I had to do was [sic] to identify and remove obstacles. The rest would follow automatically, fueled by the self-actualizing forces within the patient."

Listen to Your Inner Voice

Above all, there is a small voice inside you. That voice, however soft it may be, knows that your present emotional situation is not ideal. Your own well-being comes first, above everything else. That voice will never be as loud as your rational mind, but it might nudge you softly. It might say we need some help here, and therapy is one option. It might help you overcome some patterns of behavior that have caused you pain. This pain is no longer bearable. And it's okay to ask for help and okay to have a place where you can feel true emotions over fake happiness.

Happiness Is Subjective

Psychoanalysis is the one place left in our culture where you can be wholeheartedly unhappy. There is a pressure to be happy. . . which also means not to be unhappy. If you need to be happy, and need those around you to be happy too – it is no different than an alcoholic who needs everyone around them to drink. The problem of the happiness addict is his misery. . .

– Adam Phillips in his book On Balance

In recent times, such unabashed shows of happiness are considered toxic. Happiness has been oversold – and while we all know it is fleeting, never a permanent state of mind, we succumb to the false promises. It is one of the emotions but not all. We can consider the state of our mind to be akin to the changing seasons – on some days we could be reflective and solemn, on others exuberant and joyous. To expect and behave in a singular state of Pollyannaish glee is to deny the other natural states – and is disrespectful of the environment we could be in. Our emotional state is also a function of the environment we are immersed in. Would you jump around with joy in a global pandemic? Or choose to be a bit more measured and balanced in expressing emotions?

Mandarina11 · 18h   ...

LPT: Toxic positivity is totally a thing. Don't let the "good vibes only" people invalidate your feelings and life experiences.

Don't feel like you can't even mention the negative aspects of your life for fear of upsetting someone. You lost your job, your grandma died, you're depressed and your job search is impacting your social life?

It's perfectly normal and you should be able to discuss those "negative" parts of your life with the people close to you.

Don't ever let someone invalidate your feelings and experiences, just because they don't fit in in their fairytale idea of "positivity".

Talking about your grief can help you find support and empathy to overcome it. Talking about being unemployed and your job search can help you find a job! Talking about your problems is the way to find solutions and support.

Source: Reddit

The past century had therapy mired in social stigma, experiments, and vociferous debates. In the next century, it will be followed by more stigma, more experiments, and more debate, unless, we choose to break this cycle with fierce determination.

Bring on the Professionals!

We can start with tackling the stigma, which is the unhealthiest component. If you cannot file your own taxes, you bring in a professional who can help you. If you cannot cut your own hair, you go to a hair stylist. There is no stigma in caring for yourself. You are not broken. You don't need to be fixed. Asking for help is a way to get past some of these stumbling blocks. The therapist will gently shine light on those blocks. And you yourself will be able to leap over them. You owe it to yourself to get better. It's just like rearranging some mental furniture so that your life can flow smoothly.

MANY DIFFERENT WAYS, ONE DESTINATION

When we dig into the arc of psychological research and study, we find a number of theoretical frameworks, followed by in-fighting followed by spin-offs, leading to new models and newer techniques. Not too long ago, electric shock therapy was mainstream. Similar to our own world of start-ups, when a small group of entrepreneurs feels as though they have found a better way, they break-off from the mainstream to innovate. William Shockley may have won the Nobel Prize for inventing the transistor, but he could not keep his core team, those traitorous eight who left Shockley Semiconductor to start Fairchild. From Fairchild, a decade later came Intel. Intel laid the foundation of the 8086 microprocessor and soon followed the gamut of operating systems, databases, applications, the cloud . . . the future pulls us away from the status quo. Our ideas evolve, we perpetually improvise, and continue building upon the past. Similarly, various therapeutic techniques have evolved over time.

The three founding fathers of psychotherapy – Sigmund Freud, Carl Jung, and Alfred Adler – kicked off some key foundational techniques, and we continued to improvise over the years.

- *Psyche* – the human soul, mind, or spirit. The forces that influence our thought, behavior, and personality
- *Psychotherapy* – a dialogue between two persons, one slightly less neurotic than the other

Therapy is a structured process, as well as an art form. Laboratory experiments can be repeated with precision. But when it comes to our psyche, it is complex. Our individual experiences, our unique reactions, our belief systems and resilience – the summing up of the journey of our own souls – science cannot measure nor address these myriad complexities. Therapeutic techniques try to explore patterns of our behavior, helping us to cope better with our own idiosyncrasies. There are well over a hundred different forms of therapeutic approaches. Cognitive behavioral therapy, group therapy – a good therapist will mix and match, creating custom cocktails based on your palate and situation. Some of these may be bitter medicine, others like a cold refreshing bottle of beer after a 10-mile run.

UNCOVER THE HIDDEN AND THE REPRESSED

Having multiple therapeutic approaches is both good and bad – it has created a range of overwhelming and mind-boggling choices. But thankfully, these decisions are not to be

Table 16-1 **Knowing What We Know: The Johari Window into Our Minds**

Our Public Image (We know/Others know) Therapeutic Inquiry – What are my motivators to create this image?	**Our Blind Spots** (We don't know/Others know) Therapeutic Inquiry – How can I get honest feedback to know more? Why do I stay blind in these areas?
Our Hidden Self (We know/Others don't know) Therapeutic Inquiry – Why do I hide? Shame? Guilt? Social acceptance? Other struggles? How can I build trust with my therapist and initiate self disclosure?	**Our Unknown Side** (No one knows) Therapeutic Inquiry – How can the therapist and I collaborate in this process of discovery to find these unknowns?

made by us. We have to let the experts pick the path, similar to the way a locksmith will try a number of variants and open the keys to your unknown side. You can ask questions. You most definitely have a say in the process. You are a collaborator, but not in charge. See Table 16.1 for a look at what we know and don't know. Connecting with the right therapist is never an easy decision. The best match is (1) someone we can engage with deeply, and (2) someone we are prepared to submit to the process with and accept guidance from. Finally, we must be willing to put in the necessary effort.

The simplest outcome of any therapy is the ability to uncover your unknown side and integrate your hidden selves. The Johari window (see Table 16.1) is a fine representation of the four aspects of our selves. Founders spend a lot of time crafting their public image, some even mimicking Steve Job's like turtlenecks. But not enough time is spent uncovering the blind spots and finding out the unknown side, to strengthen and balance our inner resources. Our primary resource is the ego, so that it can work with the three tyrannical forces – (1) the id and its primal instincts, (2) the superego and its moral stance, and (3) the external social world with its fears, anxieties, and triggers.

As Freud remarked, large portions of our egos and super-egos remain unconscious – we know nothing of their contents. We need to put in an effort to make it conscious. Once we become conscious, we can build on our courage. This process of discovery starts with active collaboration and you often move from the public self to the hidden self in stages – a process of gradual uncovering, which results in some startling breakthroughs, some tears, or maybe simple findings.

THE HARD THING ABOUT THERAPY – LETTING THE THERAPIST DRIVE

Every step of this process is hard, often resulting in avoidance, our own biases, making stuff up, excuses, nonstarters, and frustrations. This becomes harder because we are not in our best states of our minds to start with. Being stressed and overwhelmed – not functioning at our prime – means we have to let go and submit to the experts. This process of letting go itself may be the hardest for entrepreneurs who have always stayed in charge. When you are no longer the conductor of the orchestra, just sitting around and letting someone else wave the baton at you will make you miserable in the short run. Every day may feel like a struggle.

Yet the only way forward is to get up every day – and start again.

Dwelling on what has been or is yet to be will not help.

Start again. Every day gives us a new chance to rebuild ourselves.

17

Stages of Therapy

Getting ready for therapy is like getting ready to invite an observant critic to come to live inside our heads for a while. A daunting premise! Before we let anyone in, we need to be prepared for hosting that person.

As the farmer tills the soil before planting seeds, so too must we get ready, be bold, make ourselves soft, open, pliable, and fertile for new ideas to take root within us. Readiness for therapy is simply getting ready for an emotional journey in which the therapist becomes your co-pilot. To start flying this machine of your mind, you need to build trust, recognize the co-pilot's skills, and get working. Your co-pilot will help to keep things on track or even help you rise up to new accomplishments – but only you can crash the plane.

FOUR PHASES OF THERAPY

Therapeutic approaches go through four phases:

1. *Acceptance – in which we emotionally identify and accept the therapist to help us.*
2. *Engagement – during which we bare our souls to the experts.*
3. *Insights and Growth – which arise after both of us work on the situation.*
4. *Development – as growth occurs, new stresses arise.*

Figure 17-1 **Therapy phases and activities.**

Acceptance (0–3 months)	Engagement (3–6 months)	Insights (6–12 months)	Development (Ongoing)
Activities: Build a cadence of meetings and communication Rapport and relationship building Understanding of techniques Early discussions of patterns	**Activities:** Build deeper trust Emotional openings Discovery of causes and blockages Crisis, anger, and resentment	**Activities:** Active involvement in between meetings Working with our dark side Objective note-taking/ feedback loops Looking at self as a third party–work in progress	**Activities:** Step functions and breakthroughs/aha moments/realizations New stresses arise as changes start to occur Sustained changes cause challenges

Check out Figure 17.1 which outlines various activities by each phase of therapy.

Step 1: Acceptance

What will make one therapist click for us over others? For some, it might be an Ivy League degree, for others, it may be a relevant experience. Have they worked with other CEOs like me? For others, the emotional bonding and gender of the therapist might take priority. If we are devout people, would it be hard for us to accept therapists who are atheists? What about if they follow a different political belief system? How do race, gender, age, nationality, or other aspects affect our subtle preferences?

What if we do not feel comfortable with our first impressions of how the therapist looks, smiles, how they shake their head, or their office wallpaper color? There might be superficial elements, but it's unlikely that we may get over them. These subtleties might pop up again and again, and we might abandon the whole process itself. As cheesy as it may sound, we have to like our therapist first, before we start this journey. Several people I spoke with struggled with the challenge of first impressions. How the therapist talked or who their features reminded them of were often dealbreakers. If we cannot feel comfortable, or accept the therapist as they are, we cannot make much progress. We will eventually share our innermost challenges with them, so trust that inner voice. This becomes much harder when access to professionals is limited, or not available easily. Depending on the geography, cultural preferences, or social pressures, we may have limited choices. In such situations, working toward acceptance is important before we get to the next stage, otherwise premature breaks can occur, causing severe setbacks.

Step 2: Engagement – or This Space Between Us

As we get past the first step of acceptance of this partnership, the engagement process starts. We build trust, open up, and start to discuss our challenges. In his poem, "A Man And A Woman Sit Near Each Other," Robert Bly writes that when two people are together, a third invisible entity is born and present. Author and therapist Dr. Irvin Yalom often asks his patients "How is the space between us today?" Speaking of this space between two people, poet Robert Bly writes:

> *as they breathe*
> *they feed someone we do not know,*
> *someone we know of,*
> *whom we have never seen . . .*

As therapists excavate the various layers of our psyches, they try to get to the crux of our beliefs, behavioral patterns, and payoffs. We discover our dark side and learn to integrate it into our daily practices.

These steps often take a lot of time – even multiple sessions. There is no short-term return on investment (ROI) here. If we start this journey expecting some magic tricks, be prepared for disappointment. Some sessions might feel like long pauses of silence peppered with just a few questions. Others may be challenging, confrontational, volatile, or weepy. But these are often termed as breakthrough sessions where we start to make progress. Those often lead to some eureka moments for the therapist. They might have struck gold – finally found that needle in our psychological haystack.

But a rich engagement brings about diligent efforts.

It took me a long time in therapy to really recognize my feelings –
anger, depression, anxiety, and sadness – and to come to terms
with them. For awhile I disowned them, seeing them as weak and
nonproductive. I often felt embarrassed, guilty, and ashamed of
having these feelings. Unfortunately, this would take me further
away from processing them and I'd dig myself deeper into the
hole. It was only over time, I was able to take more ownership of
them . . . but this was very challenging.

– Entrepreneur, 42, Los Angeles

In his best-selling book *Thinking, Fast and Slow*, Nobel
Laureate Daniel Kahneman writes that as a graduate student,
he attended courses on the art and science of psychotherapy.
During one of these lectures, his teacher shared some clinical wisdom. "From time to time I meet a patient who shares a
disturbing tale of multiple mistakes in his previous treatment.
He has been seen by several clinicians, and all failed him. The
patient can lucidly describe how his therapists misunderstood
him, but he has quickly perceived that you are different. You
share the same feeling, are convinced that you understand him,
and will be able to help." Daniel's teacher raised his voice as he
said, "Do not even think of taking on this patient! Throw him
out of the office! He is most likely a psychopath and you will
not be able to help him." Those who cannot engage well with
therapists often hop from one to another, shopping around and
deploying psychopathic charm. Therapists have been warned
to be suspicious of such patients. A patient with a repeated history of failed treatment is a danger sign, writes Kahneman. Try
not to become such a patient. The engagement and efforts are
our responsibility.

Step 3: Insights and Growth

What new perspectives will emerge – and how will you see
the world differently as you go through the process? This is
the hardest part of the therapeutic journey – the proverbial

homework our schoolteachers give us and we don't want to do it. Therapists will suggest some techniques to build into our routines, or they may have concrete tactics to add to our repertoire when certain triggers occur. As we navigate these territories with new tools, some may work and others may not. This process of finding the right tools for the myriad mental problems requires some trial and error. Are we making progress each day? Some days may be a wash, others might be two steps forward, and some may be a step backward. Putting in an honest effort, sharing factual objective information, and identifying our own progressive steps is where our true development occurs. Only with a deep sense of commitment toward our own recovery can this be achieved.

Founder's Voice

I realized that I was being manipulative and divisive, playing power games with my five direct reports. I had assumed the worst – that each of them was a power hungry maniac trying to usurp my throne and become CEO. When in fact, none of them wanted the job. It was only after several conversations and inner reflections that I realized my flawed perspective. I now no longer spend my mental cycles in fear and negativity. I have harnessed my forces to focus on customer related challenges, as opposed to being fixated on this fantastically imaginative Game of Thrones.

– CEO, San Francisco–based company

Therapists often state that *it's easier to work with those who are able to self-reflect and assume responsibility* (which I might add, is not necessarily a strength in many founders) *than it is with those who blame others for the mess they may be in.* If we do not start with a strong intention or commitment, we might end up blaming the therapist or some external entity for our own shortcomings. Remember – the therapist has no way to track or police our behavior at every step. They only know what we share with them in that session. They cannot ascertain our progress through some fact-checking mechanism. "I can only look at your role, even if it's very limited, because that's where I can be of most help," writes therapist Dr. Irvin Yalom. If we get comfortable in sharing the gory details, it can lead to progress. What worked? What did not? Can we try something else? This is only so they can be of help to us. If we make stuff up to look good in our therapy sessions and try to win the "best patient of the month" popularity contest, we are only fooling ourselves, wasting our money, time, and energy.

Step 4: Development

Is the end goal of therapy perpetual bliss? Infinite happiness? Such idealistic terms are best relegated to the romance section of the bookshelf. We might get some insights into the frustrations caused by the unfulfilled goals of our life. How have we been trying to fill these needs – directly or indirectly?

And, we can certainly seek strength and ability to cope with grace. Not all of us have the same emotional resilience. That's okay. We are all different. That's why we have therapy. D. W. Winnicott, a psychotherapist, once wrote, "therapy is complete when a child can play alone."

In one study of 2,400 patients covering 30 years of research, approximately 50% of the patients were measurably improved after eight sessions, and approximately 75% were improved by 26 sessions.

So as we start the journey, prepare for a marathon – not a one-and-done. And how do we know the work is done? We don't. We are *work in perpetual progress,* because life happens. Pandemics happen. Elections occur. Governments topple. People we love die. Lovers may leave. Start-ups explode. And we get up each day, take another step, and keep working.

18

Challenges and Pitfalls in Therapy

The hardest challenge for entrepreneurs, those who are driven by the notion of staying in charge at all times, is to let go and submit themselves. A utilitarian founder will often struggle with the intangible or subjective parts of the therapeutic process. Are we just going to sit around and talk? Give me a break; I have a company to run. Mantras like "what we cannot measure, we cannot control" will pop up. It's too fuzzy and loosey-goosey for me, one might say. Due to the subjectivity and motivations – sometimes obvious, sometimes hidden – several aspects of this entrepreneur-therapist relationship can create challenges.

Here are five challenges that often crop up in the process of working with a therapist:

Subjectivity: To start with, what we cannot measure, we cannot control. What we feel or cannot feel might be one guiding principle. If I walk into a practitioner's clinic and proclaim some symptoms of a disease – like fever or chest pain – the practitioner can measure, conduct standardized blood tests, examine lab reports, and establish the baseline and the ideal target metrics. These being clearly established, the two parties – the buyer of services and seller – then agree to work together and fix this situation. We know what success looks like. But in therapy, the diagnosis is not as simple nor can subjective states be measured easily. Although scales for measuring depression exist, such as Beck's Depression Inventory, they consist of somewhat simplistic questions that are to be self-assessed. That leads us to the second challenge.

Agency conflicts: In a self-assessed condition, we may be suffering, indeed, but the agency problem might play a curious role – the practitioner cannot verify anything but may willingly accept our self-diagnosis. In this agency, the customer is a relieved accomplice to the therapist's mental scalpel. If I am a starving therapist with no patients lining up outside the door, anyone who walks in is certainly welcome. I need to pay my bills. So sure, let's explore around for a bit. And at a very fundamental level, it may not be in the therapist's best interest to declare success. It cannot be denied that the therapist benefits financially as long as someone suffers. We realize therapists are not always taking advantage, yet we all know the realities of the world. Let us assume the best intentions to start with. On the flip side, the therapist may be willing to stick with you, work with you despite your own repetitive patterns. But if you are the nightmare of a client, can the therapist fire you?

Substitute for intimacy: In some situations, the therapist might become an outlet of sorts for the patient, a paid listener, or a substitute for intimacy. Being attached to this relationship, at times self-indulgent, may have the advantages of a confessional booth in a church. We could go every Sunday, seek forgiveness, and repeat our madness between Monday and Saturday. We will soon develop a level of intimacy because therapists are trained to listen. They do not interject, talk about their own lives, or discuss the daily news. Our intimacy develops as a result of them listening to our woes, yet this relationship cannot replace an intimate circle of friends. Sometimes, this can lead to resentment, because the therapist has many patients, whereas we each have one therapist. In our search for intimacy, we confuse a nonexclusive professional relationship for something else, thus creating challenges for both sides.

Shopping versus progressing: If the therapist recommends a tough, difficult behavioral change, and you fail to engage or put in genuine meaningful efforts, you might be tempted to look for someone who is easier to work with. The trap of staying in the shopping mall, moving from one counselor and therapist to another is yet another form of self-indulgence without progress. Once you find a therapist, stick with that person. Grit your teeth and stay in the chair as the therapist performs those painful root canal procedures with nickel titanium files. Shopping around is easy. Building the inner muscle is harder.

Asymmetric information – Selective sharing versus intellectual honesty: it all depends on what we share with our therapists. Do we exaggerate our conditions? Do we choose to slightly bend the truth or hide some details, as painful as they may be? Or, after months of progress, might we feel guilty sharing a weak moment when we succumbed to a weakness and regressed? We might fear the unspoken judgment that might come with any downturns. Yet therapists can only work with what we choose to show them – they do not have an in-house camera with a live stream. And, we may not always be able to share our harshest truths. The asymmetric information challenge – of both the problems as well as any progress – are fundamental issues that can only be addressed with intellectual honesty. French historian René Girard warns, "Psychiatry regards the sick person as a monad or a single unit. A one-off point in the continuum. The psychologist does not attach sufficient weight to the foundational character of relationships, which can cause us to swing from one point to another."

THE ROAD TO A HEALTHY MIND IS LONG

A long, wandering, sometimes painful path of nonlinear progress is a good mental model for therapy. Therapists can help identify our recurring patterns, and attempt to get rid of underlying beliefs and motivations and patterns that do not serve us well. A good therapist will then help us to build boundaries to avoid recurring patterns. The role of the therapist is to efficiently identify and dismantle all those inner blocks. This may not follow a straight line path and may often lead to frustrating dead ends. We have to commit to the process. The relationship itself will include some tough love, the building of new boundaries, and bluntly sharing the consequences of our behavior. In this process, we become aware of our fears of exploitation, abandonment or manipulation. A therapist will cut us off from our rewards mechanisms to destroy addictive loops. All this might cause, resentment, and anger – the savior turns into the devil incarnate for a while.

Digging into the past, confessing our weaknesses, embarrassments, and challenges, and prodding at wounds that may have covered up over time . . . all this can be a painful process. The therapist has no magic wand. These are like OODA (Observe, Orient, Decide, Act) loops, and we are not mute observers. We are both, the subject and the object. As we prepare for the painful process of opening up, we might turn into a helpless lump of tears and flesh. Yet our cognitive side and our active participation, willingness, and ability to experiment for our own recovery are essential for progress. Regression is normal. Long periods of silence in therapy are normal.

From an online feedback site, a review of a psychologist:

When I went to see him about a problem, he seemed completely uninterested, even giving an attitude of "why bother me with this?" He never gave an indication of understanding me or even trying. After seeing him a couple of times he asked me, "Do you really think you need to be here?" I was in a lot of psychological pain and he did not even try to understand me. Needless to say, I did not continue. I found a psychologist who was night and day better.

Breakthrough moments are rare, leading to realizations of deep-seated patterns. Often filled with elevated pain or gushing relief, these are the magical moments when the therapist has found something to extract, unlock, or shine a light on. At times, our relationship with our therapist will be filled with resentment. Therapist Dr. Irvin Yalom often asks his patients to share how they are experiencing "this space between us."

"How are you and I doing today?" he asks his patients. To nudge them to become more open, he asks, *"Imagine you get up tomorrow – how will you feel about you and me? What will be the unspoken statements or unasked questions about our relationship?"*

Therapists are human beings; they suffer burnout and depression: If a therapist becomes depressed, they may never declare it as they could lose their license. In one study, as many as 52% of clinicians report working overtime hours, resulting in feelings of alienation, burnout, and reduced work satisfaction. Additionally, mental health work is stressful, associated with emotional exhaustion and loneliness. Until the AI overlords take this profession over, let us be empathetic to the demands of this profession.

It's 3 a.m. and your robo-therapist is on standby. John, an AI-driven "therapist" algorithm built by Nick Cammarata, running on GPT-3 technology, offers support on a bad day.

> **This is a conversation between Nick and a brilliant, warm therapist named John.**
>
> **John:** Hi Nick great to see you again.
> **Nick:** I hate myself
> **John:** Wow! That sounds really bad.
> **Nick:** I'm wasting your time
> **John:** Nick you're not wasting my time.
> **Nick:** I can leave if you want
> **John:** No. I'm glad you came here today.
> **Nick:** Is there anything at all that's good about me?
> **John:** Tell me one thing.
> **Nick:** uh what?
> **John:** Tell me one thing that's good.
> **Nick:** I was okay at tennis in high school
> **John:** That's great.
> **Nick:** You should have seen my serve
> **John:** Wow, you almost sound like an athlete. And that's great. Anything else?
> **Nick:** I cook up a mean banana crepe
> **John:** That's terrific. Nick I want you to tell me why you don't think you're good?
> **Nick:** Because I suck at everything I can't even therapy well
> **John:** I'm really enjoying our time today Nick.
> **John:** We're halfway through and I feel like we've done a lot. Do you think so?
> **Nick:** Yeah :)

Source: Nick Cammarata via Twitter.

To summarize, a therapist can shine a mirror onto our hidden stumbling blocks. In doing so, we become aware of our inner friction points and can reduce these to maximize our potential. Yet, why do we resist therapy? Is it due to the stigma associated? If we called it coaching would that change the way we look at it?

Therapy is not just about controlling the downside and depression spirals. It is also a path to flourishing in life with skill and flair. The miserable can be *less miserable* and the successful can thrive to their fullest potential.

In therapy, any breakthroughs are a function of a series of experiments. They may occur in a few sessions or a few years. Only you can tell when the weight has been lifted from your shoulders. Your internal blocks have been dismantled, and you can lead a flourishing life.

19

Medicating Our Way to Recovery

When it comes to medication, two belief systems prevail. One is that the brain is a biochemical machine. All our brain activity is driven by chemistry, including thoughts, emotions, and memory. Thus, depression is a biological or chemical reaction.[1] And it has very little to do with the rest of our habits, routines, and lifestyles.

The second view looks at a lot more than just the brain chemistry. It attempts to take a more holistic and philosophical perspective. It brings in the person as well as the contextual environment. It looks at genetics, neurobiology, cognition, emotion, and social relationships. And adds external factors to that, which relate to society, macro events, and specifics, such as trauma – soon you have a pretty complex matrix.[2]

In the first belief system, that it's all just biochemistry, medications can help alleviate the mental challenges. The adjacent view – in which it is believed to be much more than just brain chemistry – often leads us to experiment with various paths to recovery. One takes a more definitive stance, whereas the other takes an experimental approach. No matter how we get there, our minds and bodies are out of tune. And we need to get back in the game. Take the example of a wounded bird or an animal in a jungle, unable to fend for itself. Chances are that it will get eaten up quickly. As humans, we do have support systems, but the very first step is to get functional or else we can spiral down.

The role of medication is a domain for professionals and best tackled by those who are trained to provide diagnosis and prescriptions. Yet a fair amount of stigma exists around the "happy pills," and their side effects. Founders were skeptical about medications and many stayed with self-care and social support groups. Let us look into why this stigma has prevailed.

THE MEDICATION DEBATE

A Harvard Medical School publication states that depression doesn't spring from simply having too much or too little of certain brain chemicals. Rather, there are many possible causes of depression, including faulty mood regulation by the brain, genetic vulnerability, stressful life events, medications, and medical problems. It's believed that several of these forces interact to bring on depression. Medications for depression are a widely debated topic, and opinions range from one extreme to another. The crux of the debate lies in the fact that no single reason – biochemical, stress, genetics – can be attributed to depression. Rather a multitude of factors can lead to depression. So while some believe medication plays a role in recovery, others believe that working with other tools may be the right path for them.

The Basics – Exercise, Sleep, and Food Habits

Founders often pride themselves in running hard, working 24/7, and always being on, always hustling. Drinking six gallons of Red Bull, caffeine, or other legal and other stimulants are rampantly deployed to fuel the all-nighters. Energy drinks and Soylent are consumed while hands are on the keyboard. A freshly prepared hot meal is a luxury or a distraction on the path to start-up success.

As mundane as it may sound, monitoring and managing the basics of our life – sleep, exercise, and food is the first step toward recovery. The merits of pulling all-nighters are overblow. Such false badges of honor lead to the rapid decline of our most precious resource – our cognitive abilities. Yet we cheer each other on and look up in awe at such stupidity. I wonder when this will stop. As a founder, you establish the boundaries, work conditions, and respect for your own body, its need for rest and recovery. If you propagate a culture of 24/7, your employees pay a huge price (while getting 0.25% of that stock option pool).

When one goes to sleep, she takes the material of this all-containing world, tears it apart, builds it back up and dreams by their own brightness, by their own light.

– from the Upanishads[3]

Web Smith ✔ @web · 3h
Mental health time:

To meet obligations, I had to go the last 40 days with very little sleep.

My health worsened to extremes. I failed to produce my best work. I strained a very meaningful partnership. I failed a lot.

I am now in the pro sleep camp. Death to hustle culture.

💬 39   ♻ 42   ♡ 812   ⬆

Source: Twitter, Inc.

As our work patterns get intense, entrepreneurs often seek solace, comfort, and escape in a range of numbing stimulants like alcohol, all of which affect the two basic anchors – namely, appetite and sleep patterns. And sometimes our cognition gets affected as well. When our sleep and appetite get out of a cadence and our basic physical needs are unmet, the downward spiral starts.

Lisa Wehden @LisaWehden · 1d ···
So much chatter about sleeping well so
I'll just say it - if you don't focus on fixing
your diet and doing regular exercise
you'll never sleep well. No app is gonna
save you.
♡ 11   ⟲ 10   ♡ 136   ⬆

Source: Twitter, Inc.

Sleeping on the Job

Like most start-ups, we were a hard-charging team of about a dozen high-energy people. We would be in the office grinding away till 11 p.m. on most days, weekends included. To sleep in the office was normal, a badge of honor. The soft acknowledgment we got the next morning was an emotional reward, one way to gain respect and attention. It was mad, patriotic, a competition – who could do more for the company. If one would die on the job they would become a martyr. During the hours of 9 a.m. to 4 p.m., we were supposed to focus on all customer-facing external activities. After 5 p.m., we did the rest – internal stuff like product roadmap, follow-up emails, content, user interface (UI), user experience [UX], and proposals and such.

This happened almost 10 years ago but I remember this vividly. One late evening over a working dinner, chowing down on some Chinese fried rice, one of us worked the whiteboard. I noticed that the founder CEO had finished his meal. And seated at the conference table, he had started to doze off, his chin dropping into his chest. While the meeting was in progress with about eight of us in the room, he had gone silent. Everyone saw and we looked at each other – awkwardly, not quite knowing what to do. After about three minutes, which seemed like eternity, he woke up with a start, looked around, a bit disoriented. And then everything resumed. It was as though we resumed a Netflix episode where we had paused. I wonder if we would have done better if we took healthy breaks from work to meet our basic biological needs. – *VP, Business, Asian start-up*

A University of Freiberg study[4] demonstrated the effect of a warm bath and its effect on depression. Eight weeks of regular warm baths scored resulted in a score six points lower on a commonly used depression scale. According to reports, baths increase the core body temperature and help synchronize our inner clock and circadian rhythms, which affect the daily fluctuations in behavior and biochemistry of our organs, including the brain. Our core body temperature falls at night, allowing for the release of melatonin. However, in depression, the temperature rhythm goes out of whack and can get delayed by several hours. The warm baths helped reestablish the baseline. Morning exposure to bright light strengthens circadian rhythms and has also been found to alleviate depression.

MOTIVATIONS, MONEY, AND THE NEED FOR SPEED

Although the overall motivations of the pharma industry are aligned with the Hippocratic oath (First, do no harm), in principle, the greater majority of companies are aiming for greater good. Yet we find some bad actors pushing for profits above patients. Not every pharma company behaves in such an egregious fashion. When short-term profit motives come into play, behavior can often get distorted. Thanks to such players, a pattern of vested interests, bias, efficacy, and side effects have tainted the pharma industry. One of the founders' repartee on this notion was, "Yeah sure, even Google wanted to do no evil, but we have seen how that plays out over time."

Vested interests – profits above people: "It is simply no longer possible to believe much of the clinical research that is published, or to rely on the judgment of trusted physicians or authoritative medical guidelines. I take no pleasure in this conclusion, which I reached slowly and reluctantly over my two decades as an editor of *The New England Journal of Medicine*," writes Harvard Medical School's Dr. Marcia Angell, author of *The Truth About the Drug Companies: How They Deceive Us and What to Do About It*. The case of Dr. Joseph L. Biederman, professor of psychiatry at Harvard Medical School and chief of pediatric psychopharmacology at Harvard's Massachusetts General Hospital was described as an example of excess. Children as young as two years old are now being diagnosed with bipolar disorder and treated with a cocktail of powerful drugs. Many drugs were not approved by the Food and Drug Administration (FDA) for such a purpose, nor for children below 10 years of age. A Senate investigation revealed that drug companies, including those that make drugs for childhood bipolar disorder, had paid Biederman $1.6 million in "consulting" and "speaking" fees.

Bias: The American Psychiatric Association's *Diagnostic and Statistical Manual (DSM)* is a reference guide that lists the symptoms that define depression and various symptoms. Some critics of the *DSM* argue that it contains sections that are subjective, poorly written, confusing, or contradictory information. One scathing observation of the work on *DSM-5*, its fifth edition, was that it "displayed the most unhappy combination of soaring ambition and weak methodology" and is concerned

about the task force's "inexplicably closed and secretive process." The members of the *DSM-5* task force were supposed to
sign nondisclosure agreements, even as 69% of the members
report having ties to the pharmaceutical industry, an increase
from the 57% from the previous edition. That the industry's

On drug discovery and research . . .

Research and Publications

- Over 50% of literature on drugs is ghostwritten /
  abnormally written.[5]
- Biased publication of antidepressant trials.[6]
- Accusations of ethical violations by leading depression researchers.[7]
- "Clinicians get presented with subsets of data, and this
  science appears in the most prestigious journals under
  the apparent authorship of leading figures . . . it has
  the appearance of science, but it is a cuckoo's egg in
  the nest of science."[8] – from a paper written by David
  Healy, published in the *British Journal of Psychiatry*.
  Healy is a professor of psychiatry and published 150
  peer-reviewed articles and 20 books, including *Phara-
  mgeddon* and *Let Them Eat Prozac*.

Transparency and Performance

- When pushed for transparency and asked to share all
  drug trials data and not just selective airbrushed data,
  pharma companies have often used court action to
  challenge such rules.[9]
- Longstanding concerns prevail about a high false-
  positive rate in diagnoses of depression.[10]
- Poor performance of antidepressants has been demonstrated in some studies relative to placebos.[11]
- Failure to improve antidepressant efficacy since the
  1950s.[12]

---

influence would aspire to sell more products is not completely out of the realm of possibility. For example, critics have voiced that certain responses to grief could be labeled as pathological disorders, *instead of being recognized as being normal human experiences*. When a public pushback occurred, changes were made to the manual and a footnote was added to the draft text, which explains the distinction between grief and depression.

Efficacy: An article in *The New Scientist* entitled "The Drugs Don't Work" addresses the challenges of depression medication squarely. Reporter Clare Wilson writes that there are 40 different drugs available for depression. Prescriptions for these drugs have increased across the board in all major countries although their mechanisms of action are mysterious. The placebo effect – its comparison to a sugar pill – continues to be debated extensively. The report describes one study in which medication showed a reduction of two points on the Hamilton Depression Scale, which measures the severity of depression across 17 parameters. In another study published in *The Lancet*, 21 antidepressants were tested and all were found to be more efficacious than placebos in adults with major depressive disorder. But the most effective drug, amitriptyline, was also on the least-tolerated list, and is generally not considered a first-line drug for depression treatment.

TO MEDICATE OR NOT TO MEDICATE IS A LONGSTANDING DEBATE

Medications work and many swear by them. And then there is the other side. You can debate the two sides ad nauseam to no end – data, sources, motivations, published papers, warring debates, studies, studies that negate prior studies, news and fake-news, and more.

But we are here to get better, not to argue endlessly. If a professional concludes that your condition may improve rapidly with medical intervention, you owe it to yourself to explore the possibility. Ask questions, do your homework, and if it does not work or side effects worsen the condition, surely raise your hand and seek alternatives. Once the professional makes a decision to prescribe medication, their goal will be twofold:

1. Alleviating the symptoms
2. Preventing the recurrence

If you subscribe to the view that drugs may not have clinical benefits, it is important to share this belief with your therapist. Some believe that medication is a sign of a character flaw, a defect, and would rather prefer some camomile tea, thank you. A range of factors can drive such views including spiritual beliefs, lack of trust of the pharma industry, concern about the economic incentives, efficacy data, drug side effects. All these reasons have led people to rely on alternatives.

Should medications be prescribed, it is alright to ask:

1. *What is the anticipated duration of the treatment?*
2. *What are any possible dependencies or addictions that may arise? When is a good time to discuss tapering-off plans? Note that not all medications are addictive. In some situations, to prevent a relapse, life-long prescriptions may be required.*
3. *What are any side effects, and how should we minimize their downside? Is there a possibility that the complexities might exacerbate my health issues?*
4. *Can they suggest any alternatives or start with lower dosage?*
5. *Are they under any pressure to prescribe drugs?*

A depressed person's analytical and cognitive faculties are not at their peak. They are vulnerable. And they come weary and helpless to the physician. The ultimate authority is a physician who can prescribe and help them recover, become productive. When the vulnerable and weak have submitted to their decisions, on occasion, physicians have not acted in the best interests of their patients. This does not taint the whole profession, yet *caveat emptor*.

Part IV

These Rituals Worked for Us

In which founders share some practices, rituals, and ways of building resilience.

20

A Soul Made Cheerful

There is one thing one has to have: either a soul that is cheerful by nature, or a soul made cheerful by work, love, art, and knowledge.

— *Friedrich Nietzsche*

Mike Maples, one of the leading investors in Silicon Valley, is generous with both his time and his tears. His is not an anger-laden theatrical bawl, loud and messy, where he snorts into three boxes of tissues, unloading his anger and fury on people around him. His tears come from the angst of watching the miasma of the founder's despair, and being unable to offer elegant solutions.

One night, at a catered dinner on the upper floors of Salesforce Tower – the tallest building west of Mississippi – Mike describes the loneliness of the founder. Speaking to a small group of a dozen investors who had just arrived in Silicon Valley, he asks, "How would you feel if what you are building is met with resistance at every step – your product, well no one cares about it . . . when you start out, your ability to attract star talent is limited – most investors cannot see the future – we all start with asking 'why,' when we should be actively co-creating the future, asking 'why not?'" His deep baritone of a voice drops to a lower note, the pace of his animated questioning has now slowed down . . . amidst long pauses, a tear trickles down his cheek. The gaggle of investors stares down in their plates, nibbling on their *tart au citron* not knowing how to react. Venture capitalists are not necessarily known for their ability to express emotions. The logical side of their brains, fueled with the daily dose of cap-tables, diligence wars, balance sheets, and analytical rigor has won the war a long time ago, and their hearts have numbed, drowned out with the intellectual chatter. Worse, they are utterly helpless in the presence of a grown man, who has invoked a sliver of their own emotional shadow, one that has been repressed by design or by the hazardous conditions of capitalistic occupation. Expressing emotions within the male of the species is a sign of confessed weakness. There is nothing to gain and we will only lose if we open up. Either we lose respect and are seen as not being a man's man, or we're taken advantage of, eaten up by the proverbial tiger in the negotiations. As a result, business meetings are devoid of emotions – positive or negative. Smiles, laughter, and tears are not encouraged at the risk of being labeled a manchild. As Mike gently weeps, we sit around, not quite sure if we should put our arms around him, offer him a box of tissue, or just pretend as though nothing has happened.

That evening, Mike taught us not only about the art of investing but a bigger lesson: when you genuinely care about founders, let it show. It's okay. It's healthy. Mike is not prone to depression, but expression. He lives his life with his soul afire, joyous and cheerful by nature. Speaking at an event in San Francisco, he once remarked that he is the worst person to talk to about depression. His daily mental state is that of gratitude, which comes as naturally as breathing oxygen. If today doesn't work out, then we try to make the most of tomorrow. And yes, at that event, which had about 600 people in the audience, Mike did shed a tear. Mike cares about everything he does – himself, his founders, his partners, and his universe. He is gifted with a soul that needs no cheering on. For the rest of us, we can cheer up our soul with work, love, art, and knowledge.

WORKING ON YOUR INSIDE – THE IMPORTANCE OF SELF-CARE

Those trapped in the deep snares of depression may find this prescription to *make your souls cheerful* to be banal. It might evoke a reaction of shrugging shoulders, asking, "So what does that exactly mean? It starts with self-care – a notion that is often dismissed by the founders.

When everything is falling apart, the last thing a depressive person needs is a menu of self-care options. "I was my own worst enemy," writes a founder. "I knew what I had to do – exercise, eat healthy, meditate, and journal – but I just couldn't get myself to do it . . . I wallowed for months and months in this stalled mode."

But Hillel the Elder reminds us, "If I am not for myself, who will be for me? If I am only for myself, what am I? And if not now, when?"

If we do not care for ourselves, like a leaky boat, we will struggle to stay afloat and work for the higher cause – to bring our mission to fruition, to shape our start-up, and work with our team. And the time to start is now. In good times, we rarely think or have the need for self-care. Drunk on life, we are celebrating each day as it comes, with neither time nor need for self-reflection. When was the last time you stopped by your doctor's office just to say, I am doing great today, would you take a look at my pulse?

Our internal state may be tempestuous or calm, but we operate in environments that are not considered normal. By choosing the path of start-up life, we are choosing to embrace chaos. If there is peace within us, the restlessness of the markets outside is trying very hard to get inside us, throw us off, or derail us. And that force is working 24/7.

The external conditions in which we choose to operate are demanding, and require us to build our inner core, our muscles. We can certainly exercise our self-care while we are in the field. Author and psychotherapist Paul Goodman once wrote that "The issue is not whether people are 'good enough' for a particular type of society; rather it is a matter of developing the kind of social institutions that are most conducive to expanding the potentialities we have for intelligence, grace, sociability and freedom."

The social forces act on us and often we do not acknowledge those triggers. If we choose to live in the social order, we strive for acceptance and conformity. Imitation becomes the modus operandi for acceptance. "Societies implant certain needs and desires in an individual and then frustrate them. Everyone is urged to get rich, while in reality, this is possible for only a few people. We are taught to want more and more – urged to be infinitely ambitious – when most of the metrics of social success are unattainable by the majority of the population," writes Abraham Maslow.

I feel insecure about my answer of "I don't know" when asked what I'll do next – that it will be viewed as inadequate.

I worry about whether I will ever do anything again that I feel as passionate about: being the Founder and CEO is the greatest job I've ever had.

I feel unsure about how others will react.

In venture, doubt isn't respected.

I am confident some, especially in VC, will inevitably view my story as a lack of grit . . .
                                        – Ryan Caldbeck, CEO, Betterup[1]

The primary reason for self-care is to help manage and deflate our own frustrations, often created by external forces – be it unfulfilled desires, manic markets, unstoppable social pressures to keep up with unicorn valuations, and maintain our station with the Joneses, their Teslas, and their IPOs. The external triggers are vast, innumerable, and can keep us on the hedonistic treadmill. But self-care is about managing the inside. Self-care falls in two categories:

1. The intentional conscious kind that drives a virtuous loop:
   • Managing states of mind – journaling, reflection, gratitude, acts of charity, or compassion

- Virtuous loops – exercise, often vigorous to get the blood flowing, burning the excess passion (and no self-flagellation), and gaining an endorphin rush,

2. Addictive autopilots, which drag us down the vicious spiral:

   - Relief from stress/rewards – eating, smoking, micro-dosing, marijuana, extramarital relationships

   - Escaping/inducing states of mind – drugs, drinking (lead to addictions and vicious cycles of poor health, work challenges, and broken families)

HOW WE AVOID SELF-CARE

Founders will assume the role of martyrs and be working all the time. "Oh no, I am building this company, which means I have to be on all the time, 24/7." That's a cop-out. Someone who does that is either lost, stressed, or flailing, and working all the time rarely solves the problem. We run away from ourselves because we cannot face our own state or the truth. Maybe things are not working and we need to take a pause. If we cannot fill our own cup, how can we lead others, or fill for others?

I have often noticed that those who have taken enough time to care and feed their own needs are able to care and feed their teams as well. To start with, watch out for the basics – food, sleep, and rest. As mama said, if we cannot get these into a routine and rhythm, we are abusing our bodies. The inner systems are unable to calibrate the timings and triggers. Unknowingly, we often fall into the escape routes – we don't know what to do with our troublesome restless states.

In such times, the low-hanging escape routes of alcohol and drugs are often the easiest paths. One of the founders wrote, somewhat tongue in cheek, that his solace comes from drinking Guinness, while meditating in an Irish bar. In fact, several founders confessed to finding temporary solace with the bottle. Yet they realized that by pulling an alcoholic curtain over a raging fire inside only blocks the view temporarily, but it does not address the problem. "Thankfully I had the aware-ness that turning to alcohol would create more problems than solutions," writes one founder.

"I was on the cutting edge. I pushed the envelope. I did the heavy lifting. I was the rainmaker. Then I ran out of metaphores."

Credit:Leo Cullum / CartoonStock

Alcohol and drugs are easy escape mechanisms and do not tackle the root cause. We may not even fully understand the root cause, but enduring this phase with some positive meth-ods is a much better option. Here is one example: "I pace the room. Eat some M&M candies. Call someone. Exercise. Go shopping. Cry under a blanket. Watch a show," wrote one founder, which is a classic approach of trying it all without get-ting too hung up. I love the simplicity and openness in which they are able to try it all.

You have to be always drunk

-by Charles Baudelaire

That's all there is to it– it's the only way.
So as not to feel the horrible burden of time
that breaks your back and bends you to the earth,
you have to be continually drunk.
But on what?
Wine, poetry or virtue, as you wish.
But be drunk.
...
It is time to be drunk!
So as not to be the martyred slaves of time, be drunk,
be continually drunk!
On wine, on poetry, or on virtue, as you wish.

21

Prescription 1 – An Organized Diminution of Work

*There was no final straw at work; frankly the
company was doing better than ever . . . It didn't
matter: I could only feel pain. My daughter looked
at me and said, "Daddy, you always look so sad."
She was five. It was the push I needed to change.*

— CEO of a venture-backed company[1]

Self-care may seem like a luxury for entrepreneurs, who
love the rush of working all the time. But considering the
grueling demands of the start-up journey, self-care should
be high up on every entrepreneur list. Busy calendars and
back-to-back-to-back commitments is all good but only if
you are thriving at each step of the way. Or as Warren Buffett
says, tap dancing your way to work. If you are struggling,
the first step is to show up, and then create some space.

PAUSE, BALANCE, BREATHE

Studies demonstrate that setting personal goals, counting your
blessings, practicing kindness, expressing gratitude, and using
personal strengths to enhance well-being can in some cases,
reduce depressive symptoms.

Founders know that despite the inner struggle, they may not be able to unplug completely and recuperate in the sunsoaked sands of Ibiza or Bali. So they show up, but try to strike a balance. Here are some voices of founders and how they dealt with the ever crashing waves of work.

- *Depression affects memory and concentration – I make lists and crossing them off gives me a sense of joy at each step. Making a list of small achievable goals. Sometimes it's just doing one thing – that's all. I tell myself I need to do just one thing that matters today. This may be making sure the bills are paid, there is enough in the bank to do payroll this cycle.*
- *Often I prepare a "perfect day" list of things I write down each day and try to get to them. On most days, it is rare that I check off each one, but it is often very fulfilling.*
- *I write down my top-three each morning and do my best to get these done by late afternoon and start to unwind. It's tough as I am a workaholic, but that's a part of my own 12-step program. If I can put things off, I do. If I can triage them, I do.*
- *Start with the tasks that you enjoy the most – that way you get in the groove and can get to the sh**ty ones with a sense of momentum. Small wins help build up confidence. Yet I also reflect on which tasks I avoid and why? Am I weak to confront it or afraid of failure? Of high expectations? Of losing? What keeps me away from these tasks?*

Creating a gap: The myth of working 24/7 has been ingrained in us. By peer pressures and the social dynamics, technological systems, and social media, our own feelings of inadequacies, or lack of options in other parts of life, we continue to row furiously toward a mythical island, brimming with fruit trees, gold, and perpetual sunshine. In our hearts, we know such a destination does not exist, yet we have no choice. Addicted to our daily rush of work, we fling ourselves in our daily routines.

I started to say no to coffee and generic meetings where someone wanted to "pick my brain" – a lot of requests kept coming in and at first I felt awful, but realized this was necessary to rebuild myself.

"A great deal of harm is being done in the modern world by belief in the virtuousness of work, and that the road to happiness and prosperity lies in an organized diminution of work," Bertrand Russell writes in his essay, "In Praise of Idleness." Here are some founders voices on dimunition of work:

- *Disconnecting completely from my work for a few hours every week, I decided to go and do something I had never done – like drive Uber – the feeling of anonymity, being of service and dealing with challenges of a logistic kind, not the intellectual kind, helped put things in perspective.*
- *I would listen to something completely unrelated to my work life – a podcast like "This American Life."*
- *I started journaling, and the act of pouring my thoughts out was a tremendous release for my internal discomfort and pressures.*

"Be patient, do nothing, cease striving. We find this advice disheartening and therefore unfeasible because we forget it is our own inflexible activity that is structuring the reality. We think that if we do not hustle, nothing will happen and we will pine away. But the reality is probably in motion and after a while we might take part in that motion. But one can't know," writes Paul Goodman. Founders who have struggled with "not-doing" share these obsevrations:

- *As a founder I was a doer, and had to learn how to delegate. I almost felt guilty asking someone to do anything for me. In that, my progress as well as theirs was hindered.*
- *I have limited my activities with the help of my team and hired a chief of staff. To be focused on my own recovery and efficiency first is my primary goal.*

- *Turn off my devices at 2100 hours and make sure I can rest well, because it never ends. And a lot of things are trying to compete with my sleep.*

Lucy Hunt @lucy_hunt · 1d
The best email signature I've ever seen:

"It is normal for me to take 2 days to read my emails and 2 more days to reflect on the matter and respond calmly. The culture of immediacy and the constant fragmentation of time are not very compatible with the kind of life I lead."

♡ 872   ⟲ 34K   ♡ 266K   ⬆

Source: Twitter, Inc.

THE FEELING OF NOT DOING

In his book *Journey to Ixtalan,* Carlos Castaneda writes about the importance of stopping the world and the supreme difficulty of hitting pause. The constant stream of overwhelming stuff – emails, to-do lists, milestones, step functions, meetings, hiring, selling . . . As a CEO, this will go on and on. As one founder told me, with an exhausted grin and a shrug, it just never stops. And self-care begins with this impossible notion of stopping the world. Do nothing. It is a strange sickness we find ourselves afflicted with – we cannot just do "nothing"; the engine has to keep running.

Many founders shared during the pandemic that, if there was a silver lining, it was the ability to pause, pull back, reflect, and take stock of their own condition. The world had actually stopped more or less. You could see everything with a new perspective, bringing about a shift in perspectives and meaning. Yet as it grinds back on, with multiple back-to-back Zoom meetings each day, the hard part is making sure that it does not grind you any more. Our work-life balance in the virtual world gets more complicated. When the physical world was paused by the pandemic, the virtual world sprang into action and it continues to go 24/7. We are doing more and doing doing doing all the time . . . "You must let your own body discover the power and feeling of not-doing," writes Castaneda. This may seem like a luxury but it is entirely possible. For those founders who took breaks, here is how the feeling of not doing starts to play out:

- *When I start slipping down the road toward negative self-talk and darkness, I take time to breathe, slow down, and ask if I'm respecting myself in the situation. I've learned that a big part of my burnout was bad communication and spending too much time dwelling on other people's expectations and my own past mistakes – posted on hackernews.*

- *Taking several breaks during the day, to take a deep breath, to reflect on what I am grateful for is one way I keep going.*

- *Taking frequent walks to clear my mind and rebuild my focus.*

- *Making sure I do not get too excited or too discouraged at the course of events.*

- *As founders, so much is out of our control, and so I try to make sure I can truly enjoy things I HAVE control over – these are simple activities like exercising or cooking.*

22

Prescription 2 – Get Out of Your Head

Like a room we may have occupied for too long, we may be too much in our heads, dwelling, ruminating, and spinning around. To get out of the head and move in the body sounds like a prescription that the shamans, sages, and reiki masters might offer. It's easier said than done, but the body does have a magical way of slowing down that overactive mind.

LESS HEAD, MORE BODY

Philosopher G. K. Chesterton writes, "It is the logician who seeks to get the heavens inside his head. And it is his head that splits. Madness dwells not in irrational minds but in rational ones that overestimate what they can grasp," he warns.

Our mind has moved to the clouds – not the Amazon cloud but the one with too many ideas, fantasies, and self-absorption – and we seek to bring it down into the gravitational pull of our bodies.

One of the first steps toward "getting out of the head" and into the body ties to our breathing patterns. Notice if your breathing is shallow, irregular, unsteady in any way. "The relationship between our breath and our mind is like that of a mother and child," writes B. K. S. Iyengar, in his treatise of breath techniques, *Light on Pranayama*. When the mind is agitated, like a restless baby, deep breathing techniques can often calm it down. A steady breath can bring the mind into a state of relaxation.

A founder described that they would find their own breathing patterns to be very erratic. When tensed, which was most of the day, they would tend to hold their breath and clench their fists, their shoulders tightened up, like a frightened animal. Studies have shown the prevalence of anxiety and depression in persons with chronic breathing disorders. In fact, enough evidence exists to show a link between breathing disorders and depression.

So one of the simpler techniques to work with would be to start filling up those lungs. Be it walking, running, or other forms of exercise.

Burn It Up

The majority of the founders and CEOs surveyed expressed that it was "running, hiking . . . physical exercise" that helped them tremendously. "I just throw on my shoes and run for 30 to 70 minutes," shared one founder. "When I get back and sit in my chair, I always feel better. A daily run and measured progress gives me a sense of daily accomplishment." And multiple studies show the benefits of exercise on our mental states.

Exercise can prevent the development of stress-related mood disorders, such as depression and anxiety. The underlying neurobiological mechanisms of this effect, however, remain unknown.

Although physical exercise for the stressed is easy to prescribe, to build a disciplined regimen can be a drudgery. Most of us just want to stay in bed for the better part of the day. "I wish I could commit to 100% for my practice but it's harder to do during a depressive bout," writes one founder.

But very soon the notion of exercise can become a double-edged sword, cutting back into the very root causes. "I am a competitive triathlete and noticed that running was putting me in a competitive mode, increasing my stress levels.

I decided to balance this out and pay attention to my sleep patterns instead," writes a founder. For some, it was hard to get out of bed. For others, the hyperactivity needed to be tuned down. Ah . . . the quest for balance in everything we do.

Solvitur ambulando – It Is Solved by Walking

Random walks, nature hikes, and the Japanese way of forest bathing offer the opportunity to pause and step back. "The moment my legs begin to move, my thoughts begin to flow" Thoreau once said. The pull of a forest and the mountains can be rejuvenating and healing in many ways. John Muir writes that in going out, he was really going in.

"I'd take a day in a week and head out to the woods," shares a founder. "I'd walk for hours while on conference calls." And during the pandemic, this was a default way for many to find some calm in nature. Hiking, backpacking, and camping have their own advantages.

In *Backpacking with the Saints: Wilderness Hiking as Spiritual Practice*, author Belden C. Lane shares that he does not seek escape or exercise in the wilderness, but a spiritual depth of intimacy. "I am moved by nature's power and beauty," he writes. A practice in Japan, called forest bathing, encourages people to simply spend time in nature, be among giant trees, and soak in their presence – no actual bathing required. No trail runs, roughing it out on mountain bikes, or intense hikes. Be in the moment, catch the silence, the sounds, the fresh air – immerse your senses.

In a forest-bathing study conducted across 24 forests, a 15- to 20-minute walk showed positive impact across six parameters – lower concentrations of cortisol, lower pulse rate, lower blood pressure, greater parasympathetic nerve activity, and lower sympathetic nerve activity. In another similar study, subjects were exposed to a sequence of 30 scenes projected on a wall while exercising on a treadmill. Although exercise alone significantly reduced blood pressure, increased self-esteem, and had a positive significant effect on four of six mood measures, both rural and urban pleasant scenes produced a significantly greater positive effect on self-esteem than the exercise-only control. This shows the synergistic effect of *green exercise* in both rural and urban environments. Green exercise has important public and environmental health consequences, the researchers concluded.

- *Salivary cortisol was significantly lower in the forest area; over 15% decrease after the walking. Moreover, the average pulse rate and average blood pressure – both systolic and diastolic – were significantly lower in the forest setting.*
- *Parasympathetic nerve activity, which promotes rest and digestion (unlike the sympathetic nerve activity, which triggers fight or flight) was enhanced in the forest settings by over 100% after walking in a forest area.*
- *Sympathetic nervous activity decreased by about 20% when the subjects were walking in or viewing a forest.*

As many as 10 separate studies have consistently shown such results. But just as meditation does not do it for some, a forest walk may not do it for you. Maybe a walk in the city itself would work for you? "During my dark period, I would go on long manic walks through crappy parts of New York City," writes one founder. Interestingly, in a paper titled "Urban Street Tree Biodiversity and Antidepressant Prescriptions," published in *Nature*, researchers found lower rates of antidepressant prescriptions for people who lived in higher density areas of street trees. The study suggests that *unintentional daily contact with nature* through street trees close to the home may reduce the risk of depression.[1]

SILENCING THE INNER CHATTER

Author Yuval Noah Harari goes for 30-day silent meditation retreats, sometimes twice in one year. And I cannot sit silently for one hour. I am often reminded of poet Pablo Neruda, who wondered why we keep our lives moving. If we could do nothing, a huge silence might interrupt our sadness, he warns – a sadness of never understanding ourselves. Neruda pities the busy body and urges us to do nothing for once, so that we can understand ourselves.

Much has been written about yoga and stilling our minds. Much has been written about it for 400 years, yet we still struggle. We know what to do. The harder part is the discipline of doing it. Not just experimenting with it, dabbling, or feeding our curiosity, but building a daily practice. It really could be any practice – our challenge lies in crafting a daily routine, whether it is sitting on a mat, slowing down our inner critic, that relentless self-beration. Focusing on our breathing . . . all of it is much harder to do on a regular cadence. The first time is novelty and curiosity, but the eighth time is when the routine begins, and most of us get bored, are not as persistent, or get attracted by the next cool thing. Gym memberships spike in January and taper off in March. The novelty is gone but the pain and problems persist. The easy alternatives soon emerge. "The lazy way out is to indulge in drugs, alcohol, or sex," one founder told me, "but all of the good stuff . . . oh man, it is tough work."

And in such states of mind, it is better not to aim too high and get frustrated, but to start with baby steps.

In the dark noon of my struggle, I found solace in elementary yoga largely because of the gentle teacher whose very presence imbued a sense of peace and calm in me. Our class was about a dozen people. We would sit in a silent cross-legged pose for what felt like eternity. My mind would slowly come to a stop. On some days, this felt like hours, when it was no more than 15 minutes and I would lose sense of time. The next 90 minutes would become a crescendo of sorts, where our poses, intensity, and pace would vary, culminating in a final pose called savasana, where we would lie like dead bodies. In the middle of my depression, I was able to do the headstand – my life had figuratively turned on its head. The pose was merely a reflection of that reality.

– Founder

MANAGING THE VELCRO OF NEGATIVE EXPERIENCES

In the book *Buddha's Brain: The Practical Neuroscience of Happiness, Love, and Wisdom,* authors Rick Hanson and Richard Mendius describe the brain's chemistry, its impact on human psychology, and the effects of meditation. "Our brain is like Velcro for negative experiences," they write. Our brains are wired to acquire feelings of negativity and helplessness from a few failures, but it is hard to undo these feelings, even with many successes. Bad information carries more weight than good, our losses hurt more than the joys of our wins and it takes five positive interactions to overcome the effects of a single negative one. The authors extol the virtues of meditation supported by scientific evidence that it increases gray matter in the brain and builds up our attention, compassion, and empathy. It decreases stress, strengthens the immune system, and helps cardiovascular disease, asthma, diabetes, and chronic pain.

Best of all, meditation can help with numerous psychological conditions including insomnia, anxiety, phobias, and eating disorders. Meditation techniques are not in short supply, whether it is Transcendental Meditation practiced by Ray Dalio, or Vipassana meditation practiced by Jack Dorsey. There are a number of options; some work for us, others don't. But they're worth trying.

I went into a deep depression and did not have access to resources like therapy and medication. I had nothing else to turn to and threw myself into meditation as my one final lifeboat . . . it transformed my life completely, which I never anticipated."
*   – Author and comic book artist Yumi Sakugawa*

Jack Dorsey, CEO of Twitter, tries Vipassana, the 10-day silent meditation:

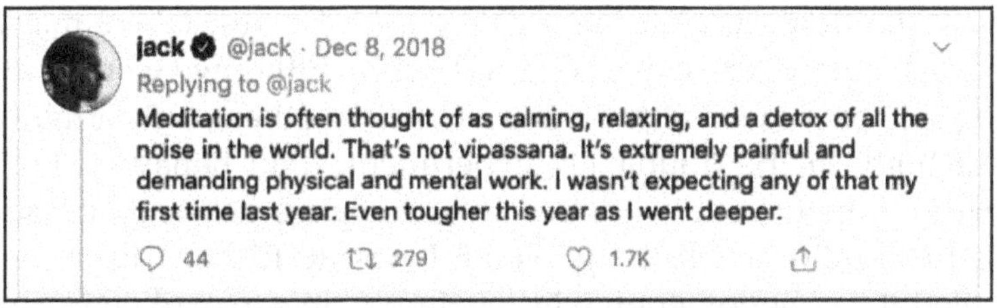
jack @jack · Dec 8, 2018
Replying to @jack
Meditation is often thought of as calming, relaxing, and a detox of all the noise in the world. That's not vipassana. It's extremely painful and demanding physical and mental work. I wasn't expecting any of that my first time last year. Even tougher this year as I went deeper.
44 279 1.7K

Source: Twitter, Inc.

Although yoga's twin activity is often perceived as meditation, and the two are used in the same sentence, these are quite far apart in form and function. Yoga strengthens the vessel, our bodies, and prepares them for mental functions like mindfulness and concentration. Meditation does not come easy for the depressed, often leading to worsening inner criticism.

- *How do I sit still?*
- *What should I do with myself? I am used to having my daily to-do lists, always in motion. Is that just another form of addiction?*
- *How do I stop my thoughts? The machine keeps whirring. This is exhausting.*
- *Am I doing this right? Should I focus on my breath? Or my third eye?*
- *Am I fidgeting too much?*

No one knows if we are doing it right. But as they say, the only bad meditation is the one we could not do at all.

The Observer and the Observed

The importance of meditation and observing yourself – being the meta observer – can be best emphasized from an example from particle physics. In the world of quantum mechanics, the famous double-slit experiment showed that matter and light behave as both particles and continuous waves. Historically, we knew it was either a particle – which is like a discreet butterfly floating around on its own – or waves, where many particles are interconnected and flowing. Either we were floating solo or we were attached to a bunch of others, but certainly not both. In the double-slit experiment, light behaves like a particle or a wave, and this interchanging behavior causes us to question everything. Nobel Laureate Richard Feynman called it "a phenomenon which is impossible to explain in any classical way . . . the only mystery of quantum mechanics."

And what is more interesting, the behavior of the particles changed when being observed, just as we change our behavior when someone is watching us. And so in meditation, while the observer and the observed are one, we are trying to observe ourselves and our mind. Eckhart Tolle writes that the beginning of freedom is the realization that you are not the thinker. Knowing this enables you to observe the entity. The moment you start watching the thinker, a higher level of consciousness becomes activated.

We are merely trying to go inside our own psyche. We might just change our behavior when we are being observed. One of the founders writes, "I enjoyed meditation and found so much relief . . . maybe I should start my next company around it." To start with, technology can come to the rescue. A number of apps can help – soothing voices and chants that can put us in a calmer state – or timers to help us build our daily practice.

CORTISOL, SEROTONIN, AND DOPAMINE – THE MAGIC OF TOUCH

Studies have shown that during massage therapy, our cortisol levels, the primary stress hormone, fall by as much as 30%, while serotonin (which stabilizes our moods) and dopamine (which recognizes pleasure) increase by about 30%.

But for some, the very notion of a stranger's touch is like an attack to the machismo pride. The mere act of flopping on a massage table for an hour, letting go, submitting yourself to someone who will knead their knuckles in your lower back may release all kinds of suppressed emotions.

When I asked one founder, she told me that she feel vulnerable in such settings, and on one occasion during massage therapy, her tears started to flow. "I have no idea what it triggered in me – it was awkward to lie there face down and sob. I was trained not to show emotions, and am afraid to be perceived as weak and then be taken advantage of."

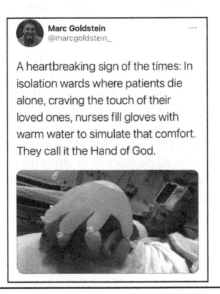

Marc Goldstein
@marcgoldstein_

A heartbreaking sign of the times: In isolation wards where patients die alone, craving the touch of their loved ones, nurses fill gloves with warm water to simulate that comfort. They call it the Hand of God.

Source: Twitter, Inc.

Most of us are deprived of human touch, the basic form of human bonding, care, attentions, or love. The fist bump or a simple handshake seems like a luxury in the post-COVID era. As the world opens back up, this simple human touch may work well for some. The 30% drop in cortisol and the 30% dopamine bump is worth every minute of this magic.

This is what you shall do – Walt Whitman

This is what you shall do; Love the earth and sun and the animals, despise riches, give alms to every one that asks, stand up for the stupid and crazy, devote your income and labor to others, hate tyrants, argue not concerning God, have patience and indulgence toward the people, take off your hat to nothing known or unknown or to any man or number of men, go freely with powerful unedu-cated persons and with the young and with the mothers of families, read these leaves in the open air every season of every year of your life, re-examine all you have been told at school or church or in any book, dismiss what-ever insults your own soul, and your very flesh shall be a great poem and have the richest fluency not only in its words but in the silent lines of its lips and face and bet-ween the lashes of your eyes and in every motion and joint of your body.

23

Prescription 3 – Feeling, Not Thinking

You are the Captain of this ship. You have no right to be vulnerable.

– *Mr. Spock,* Star Trek

I urge you to please notice when you are happy and exclaim or murmur or think at some point, "If this isn't nice, I don't know what is."

– *Kurt Vonnegut,* A Man Without a Country

A state of flow comes when we are deeply immersed in any favorite activity. Like that runner's high, we lose the space-time context. We find ourselves exhilarated, filled with a kind of refreshing joy and feeling that words can barely describe.

For some, it comes from music.

For others it's art.

Carl Jung would often pick up a hammer and a chisel, carving stone as a way to engage with his muse. In one situation, Jung writes, "The story of how this stone came to me is a curious one. I needed stones for building the enclosing wall for the garden. But when the stones were delivered, instead of a triangular stone, a square block had been sent. The mason was furious and told them to take it right back. But when I saw the stone, I said, "No, that is my stone, I must have it!" I wanted to do something with it. Only I did not yet know what.

Jung goes on to inscribe words that came to him, one after the other, in a state of flow as he chiseled away. He writes that he is an orphan, a youth, an old man – all at the same time. He is in the woods, the mountains, and the innermost soul of man. Mortal, yet untouched by cycle of eons. The words that flowed from him – on his stone, the one he had to have – have now become a paean of his life's work.

"When the stone was finished, I looked at it again and again, wondering about it and asking myself what lay behind my impulse to carve it," recalls Carl Jung. None of his words were scripted. The words came in a state of flow.

As we look at ways we get into "feeling" mode and get out of the "thinking and analyzing" mode, here are a few paths to explore, whether its poetry, immersing yourself in music, artistic endeavors, gratitude journals or volunteering. In each of these paths, you are getting away from the ruminations of your condition, including those two imposters that plague us: (1) why me? and (2) what about me?

POETRY IS FEELING – NOT THINKING

Poet E. E. Cummings writes that poetry is feeling – not knowing or believing or thinking. No more head, only heart. Author and CEO Coach Jerry Colonna often reads poetry aloud to entrepreneurs, immersed in the experience of rich emotions that come with each word, uttered slowly and relished, as we might slowly indulge in a piece of dark chocolate. Amidst the pandemic, at one virtual gathering of lost founders, he reads *Old Maps No Longer Work* by Joyce Rupp, each line delivered as a gentle dose. When the world was shut down, and we were all lost, confused, sad, and irritated, when no one quite knew what the new normal would be, Jerry brought out some soul food. No promises were made, nor any sugary syrup poured. The recitation merely acknowledged that the world around us had changed. Our beliefs, actions, patterns of behavior and daily routines of work, our commute, travel, and everything we did was changing. And we had to change with it. We had to let go. We had to trust the darkness and read our path by the stars that shine within us.

For the restless, poetry therapy can often be a gentle balm, a way of calming down the flitting minds. If we thumb through the timeless masterpieces or those newly minted, words have the power to move us. Lebanese poet Khalil Gibran's *The Prophet* has a page for every human condition, yet is succinct and heartwarming. The Persian poet Jalaluddin Rumi speaks of the heart like no other. Emily Dickinson and T. S. Eliot were giants for their time and in recent years, Garrison Keillor's compilation of *Good Poetry for Hard Times* or Rupi Kaur's *Milk and Honey* has a staggering 16,000 reviews on Amazon.

Rumor has it that when founders would be lost, venture capitalist Bill Gurley would go over and sit them down, pour a drink, and read them lines from Rudyard Kipling's poem "If." The therapeutic balm of a confidant who cares, mixed with the timeless wisdom of Kipling's poem can bring much relief. Here is an excerpt that shines as a eulogy in the memorial service of any dead company to pacify its grieving founders.

> ... *If you can meet with Triumph and Disaster*
> *And treat those two impostors just the same;*
> *If you can bear to hear the truth you've spoken*
> *Twisted by knaves to make a trap for fools,*
> *Or watch the things you gave your life to, broken,*
> *And stoop and build 'em up with worn-out tools:*
> *If you can make one heap of all your winnings*
> *And risk it on one turn of pitch-and-toss,*
> *And lose, and start again at your beginnings*
> *And never breathe a word about your loss;*

Silicon Valley venture capitalist and author Ben Horowitz finds his mojo in rap music – a different form of poetry. Poetry often helps us to hear what we need to hear, relate to expressions of poets, and find our own meaning within. A poet's work is a finer rendition of their own angst, and by expressing these elegantly, they bring voice to the unspoken frustrations of our society.

A poet is somebody who feels, and who expresses his feelings through words. This may sound easy. It isn't. A lot of people think or believe or know they feel – but that's thinking or believing or knowing; not feeling. And poetry is feeling – not knowing or believing or thinking. Almost anybody can learn to think or believe or know, but not a single human being can be taught to feel. Why? Because whenever you think or you believe or you know, you're a lot of other people: but the moment you feel, you're nobody-but-yourself. To be nobody-but-yourself – in a world which is doing its best, night and day, to make you everybody else – means to fight the hardest battle which any human being can fight; and never stop fighting –

– E. E. Cummings

MUSIC AND MOODS

One of the founders writes, "When things would get over-whelming, I would lose myself in the strumming of a guitar. My mind would be jumping around on a hundred to-dos and my guitar helps me to put things in perspective. I play for a few hours . . . I play a lot and am even getting good at it." Playing an instrument is an active way to shift the inner states. In studies, music has been found to reduce pain, anxiety, and depression of patients during operative procedures and after heart surgeries, such as coronary artery bypass grafting.

Music streaming site Spotify has 275 million monthly active users, each of whom averages about 25 hours of streaming each month. Fifty million tracks can be streamed, and Spotify API offers a happiness score, called valence, to each track. Tracks with high valence sound more positive (e.g., happy, cheerful, euphoric), whereas tracks with low valence sound more negative (e.g., sad, depressed, angry) according to Spotify. The higher the score, the happier the song. For example, Aretha Franklin's "Respect" scores a 97 out of 100, whereas Radiohead's "Creep" gets a 10.

After analyzing 330 billion streams of happy songs and seasonal patterns, *The Economist* came to some pretty interesting observations of music and our moods. Across the globe, the gloomiest time is late January and early February. The gloom drop of our collective moods occurs across the globe and even in countries like Australia and Singapore, where we cannot blame the winter. July is the perkiest month, maybe due to the summer spike.

Another interesting slice of the data comes from geography. Latin America on average listens to a lot of happier music all year round. Finland sees the biggest swings between perkiest (when the sun is shining) to the gloomiest (when the clouds come to stay). What this study shows is rather fascinating. Our moods and music are also tied to an annual calendar, where our general sense of well-being ebbs and flows.

Collaborative songwriting is yet another technique that has worked well in tackling stress disorders.

We were not designed to be happy at all times and as we respect these ebbs and flows, we come to appreciate the dark nights as well. Our self-care need not change dramatically in February. We realize everyone is in a funk, it's time to reach out proactively, be a bit more supportive, to reflect and go inward, and stay connected to our innermost circle of kind-loving people . . . because, well, when everyone is in a funk we have to remind ourselves that this too shall pass.

IN SERVICE OF OTHERS

As hard as it may be to step outside our own darkness and serve others, volunteering is prescribed, suggested, and healthy – a form of service that helps us to empathize, support, and nurture others while getting out of our own heads. A study of over a 1,000 participants with serious mental illness showed that volunteers reported better health as compared to those who did not. Other studies have affirmed that people who volunteered less had more pain, lower perceived life purpose, more depressive symptoms, and decreased physical activity. This study even quantified that approximately 9% of the relationship between pain and depression can be accounted for by volunteering.

My therapist recommended that I volunteer for the suicide hotline. I did not feel ready for this and felt it was too much to do, even as I was trying to deal with my own situation. After a bit of coaxing, I mustered up enough courage and signed up. I went through a six-week training program before I could take any calls. I realized that my ability to listen and gently support the callers gave me both a sense of purpose and perspective. That my problems seemed so miniscule in comparison. That was one way I could get out of my funk, but I also realized that the world is a much larger complex place. Everyone is fighting a battle of some kind and my perspectives evolved as I volunteered. This is definitely not for everyone – but for those who can help others in anyway, I strongly recommend it.

– Start-up employee, North Carolina

GRATITUDE WITH PRESENCE

Stronger feelings of gratitude are associated with lower draw to materialism, and improved well-being. Gratitude journals, acts of gratitude, expressions of gratitude are all essential fodder for our souls.

One of my co-founders, a devout practitioner of Islam, explained that when he prays five times a day, he expresses gratitude for as many as 33 different gifts at each time of prayer. Which means he expressed gratitude for over a 150 different events and acts each day.

I could barely come up with 10 things to be grateful for. A rough reminder that I had lost my gratitude muscle and had started to take everything for granted. The air we breathe, the water we drink, our health, friends and social systems. . . In my depressed state of mind, none of these were gifts, but assumed as entitlements.

I soon realized that I was missing out on one of the subtlest nuances of life – that being grateful is an act of submission, an act of receiving, gifts and grace which flow from other sources. Gratitude is not for those who seek power. It is for those who know that we live in a deeply interdependent world and everything is connected.

– Founder, San Jose, California

Although there are plenty of Instagram reminders and motivational posters to "be grateful," one study shows that the moment we go into a habitual auto-pilot of saying "thanks" without expressing it from the heart, its benefits vanish. So while motivational gurus will urge you to be grateful, and express gratitude at every step, know that if you do it without the depth of feelings, and get into an auto-pilot mode, it is a wasted effort. The act of gratitude that truly matters is the one that arises from the innermost sinews of your heart.

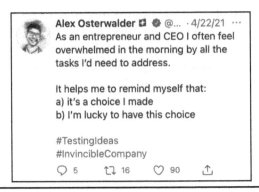

Source: Twitter, Inc.

IT'S A MATTER OF TIME – REFLECTIONS AND RUMINATION

Worry and anxiety are two big symptoms and causes of depression, writes Alex Korb, in his book *The Upward Spiral: Using Neuroscience to Reverse the Course of Depression, One Small Change at a Time*. When I asked about avoiding rumination, many founders simply stated that they had no idea how to avoid it completely. "It's a daily battle. I struggle keeping it all together," some said. Naturally, they were in a state of shambles. To ask how they'd get off such a state was unfair and insensitive. The challenge of our condition is that we only pause to reflect *when our capacity to reflect may be at its lowest*. Yet, we have to start with reflection. Not letting it turn into self-absorption or self-flagellation. Just enough time to observe, appreciate, and course correct.

A physics buff shared his course-correction tactic quite simply as follows: "Space and time are the foundation of all theories and we just have to let this time go by." When I asked him about space, he promptly grinned and added, "Oh – this space – Silicon Valley sucks because we constantly compare ourselves with others." He pointed out that the social construct and geography does have an effect on his own well-being. "In getting away from the madness of Silicon Valley, I find that the theater of the absurd no longer affects me – I am no longer of it, but still pursuing my dream."

24

Prescription 4 – Spirit over Mind

Spirituality – *the quality of being concerned with the human spirit, as opposed to material or physical.*

To be concerned with the human spirit, your own spirit – as we step toward healing and recovery – can be an unsettling notion. For the logically oriented, the notion of spirit can be a turnoff. Spirituality, often associated with organized religion, has become a stigma in parts of society where reason is worshipped.

STARING IN THE ABYSS

Thanks to the prescriptive nature of organized religion, abuses of power, and logical advancements, we live in a day and age that has no room for the mysterious. With the excessive push within some religious sects to inculcate fear and attract blind followers, the pendulum has swung to the extreme. We have run away from it all. Spirituality has turned into power games, bizarre cults, and manipulations.

Yet the role of the spiritual and the many ways it can be therapeutic cannot be ignored nor denied.

Every man, whether he is religiously inclined or not, has his own ultimate presuppositions. He finds he cannot live his life without them, and for him they are true. Such presuppositions, whether they be called ideologies, philosophies, notions, or merely hunches about life exert creative pressure upon all conduct.

– Gordon Allport

Surely, spirituality is not a substitute for treatment. Yet it has the possibility of augmenting recovery. In accepting our spirituality, we also express:

- *A form of gratitude for the beauty we see and experience around us.*
- *A break away from the rat race puts things in perspective, be it Sunday, Sabbath, or a time of contemplation.*
- *A petition to empathize with and help others who may be in pain – getting out of our head and our needs. As one founder remarked, their vacation to Vietnam changed the way they saw their own "first-world" problems.*
- *A belief in something bigger, something mysterious, more than what meets the logical.*

Spirituality is an extension of our beliefs, those that are tied to a sense of inner peace and contentment. Some describe that as bliss, rapture, or nirvana. Depending on the belief systems, you might find that art and solitude gives you that peaceful feeling. For others, it is a run, or sitting quietly in meditation. The symbols and artefacts we use to achieve the inner state does not matter. What matters is getting to that inner state. It is a high of a different kind.

Look again at that dot. That's here. That's home. That's us. On it everyone you love, everyone you know, everyone you ever heard of, every human being who ever was, lived out their lives. The aggregate of our joy and suffering, thousands of confident religions, ideologies, and economic doctrines, every hunter and forager, every hero and coward, every creator and destroyer of civilization, every king and peasant, every young couple in love, every mother and father, hopeful child, inventor and explorer, every teacher of morals, every corrupt politician, every "superstar," every "supreme leader," every saint and sinner in the history of our species lived there – on a mote of dust suspended in a sunbeam.

Our posturings, our imagined self-importance, the delusion that we have some privileged position in the Universe, are challenged by this point of pale light. Our planet is a lonely speck in the great enveloping cosmic dark. In our obscurity, in all this vastness, there is no hint that help will come from elsewhere to save us from ourselves.

– Carl Sagan, Pale Blue Dot: A Vision of the
Human Future in Space

If you choose any path, do it only for enriching your soul – we often make it a social act, to impress your virtues upon others. The advantages of community and the weekly rhythms of shifting our emphasis from the mundane to the mystical are undeniably powerful. It can be a salve for inner chaos.

WHAT DO YOU WORSHIP?

"There is no such thing as not worshiping. Everybody worships. The only choice we get is what to worship," writes David Foster Wallace. "If you worship money and things, if they are where you tap real meaning in life, then you will never have enough."

This notion of a God, spirit, a higher power – what we can neither see nor measure – can get many scientific minds into a spirited (pun intended) debate. To which we can say, even the diehard atheists may have occasionally experienced a small miracle – something that defies logical constructs. And the most devout have moments when they wonder if God truly exists. Atheism, monotheism, agnostics, and the rest have found something to anchor upon. In the East, the notion of worship takes a multitude of forms – in inanimate stones, or trees, elephants, and such. When I asked a person who worshipped a stone idol, she spoke sternly, as if chiding a wayward child and said, "It is no different from going to a gym. I am merely exercising my sense of wonder and gratitude." Picking the right Gods is a choice you can make.

PICK YOUR GODS OR THEY PICK YOU

When the logical and practical fail to answer some of our questions or to address the challenges, we often turn to the mystical and unknown. Steve Jobs traveled to India in his younger years, read *The Autobiography of a Yogi*, connecting to the spiritual in his own way.

Pat Gelsinger, CEO of companies like Intel and VMware, has authored two books – a highly technical nerdy programming guide to the 80386 microprocessor and a book about the role of Jesus in his life. In *The Juggling Act: Balancing Your Family, Faith, and Work,* Pat writes about the importance of spirituality and religion in his work.

Attributing his success to God and Jesus Christ, Pat writes that if he had been born earlier in the family, he would have been a farmer. But because his older brothers got their share of the family farm, not much was left for him and he pursued a path in the world of technology, meeting his wife at a Bible study group. When Andy Grove, the former CEO of Intel would swear and scream, Pat bluntly told him to not take the "Lord's name in vain." For Pat, his relationship with God comes above everything.

A number of founders described their own mental health challenges and shared that God, religion, prayers, a higher purpose, or just sitting in an empty church have helped them. Others write about their faith and spirituality coming to their rescue. "I prayed and read my Bible every morning, crying out to God, asking Why? In the Bible, I found stories of people enduring through difficult times, and persevering, which helped me to persevere as well," writes one founder.

Accepting the presence of a higher power, be it from our meditations or from the lessons that come from Bible, the Koran, the Bhagavad Gita, or the Visuddhimagga, the end goal is the same – to find solace, resilience, and integrity of our head, heart, and soul.

As one founder shared, "I am a fairly utilitarian person and such notions of God and spirituality are outside my grasp. But I thought – what do I have to lose? Nothing. That I can give this a try was really easy, and once I let my inner barriers drop, I found a new port – like 80 or 443 – opening up in my operating system." In computer networks, ports 80 and 443 are used to access the internet. And for this founder his own relief came after his views about his situation started to change.

A Lakota Indian Prayer – Chief Yellow Lark

Oh, Great Spirit, whose voice I hear in the wind, whose breath gives life to all the world.
Hear me; I need your strength and wisdom.
Let me walk in beauty, and make my eyes ever behold the red and purple sunset.
Make my hands respect the things you have made and my ears sharp to hear your voice.
Make me wise so that I may understand the things you have taught my people.
Help me to remain calm and strong in the face of all that comes towards me.
Let me learn the lessons you have hidden in every leaf and rock.
Help me seek pure thoughts and act with the intention of helping others.
Help me find compassion without empathy overwhelming me.
I seek strength, not to be greater than my brother, but to fight my greatest enemy, Myself.
Make me always ready to come to you with clean hands and straight eyes.
So when life fades, as the fading sunset, my spirit may come to you without shame.

SEEKING SOLACE

Yet like every other prescription, no one size fits all. For some, being in nature can heal; for others, singing in a choir on Sunday. Some may choose to be quiet and contemplate while others might find solace in the company of dear friends. Some find peace in nature. Some find it in music. Some find it in silence. Some find it in vigorous exercise. You have to find what works best for your unique psyche.

There are no moral judgments if you don't seek spiritual solace or pray. Thankfully, in some parts of the world, this is no longer a social issue. No ostracism if you do not follow the crowds or practice certain activities on Sundays. You and your God are your private business, which is exactly the way it should be. Spiritual shopping – hopping from one set of beliefs to another – is fine, but caution: the process of shopping itself can become a fun game for feeding our curiosity. It's good to explore. But exploring is not the goal. Going deeper requires you to sit still. And dig into our darker side.

UNDERSTANDING OUR SHADOW SIDE – FEARS, ENVY, RESENTMENT

You can torture out "shadow" reasons all you want, but it's really deflecting from the big obvious fact that un-live-with-able circumstances are un-live-with-able . . . you need to actually fix and remove traumatic circumstances. You should not endorse "being resilient" to them . . .
        – From hackernews, *an online forum for entrepreneurs*

In *Owning Your Own Shadow*, Robert A. Johnson writes, "The word suffer comes from the Latin *sub plus ferre*, meaning to bear or to allow." Jung reminds us, "the development of the personality is one of the most costly of all things." How should we bear witness and engage with our dark side? And what cost do we pay?

Just as each of us has a unique fingerprint, our dark side is different for each one. Qualities such as egotism, laziness, sloppiness, unreal fantasies, schemes, and plots; cowardice; inordinate love of money and possessions . . . Jung warns that when we see these elements within us and come to terms with our dark side, shame and guilt can creep in. We can get confused and paralyzed. This is a price we pay, but can be a temporary haze. Once we realize that such elements are sprinkled generously and in unequal parts within all of us, we can start to inch along. When we start to dig inside and excavate our personas, the process can be unsettling. We may find that we are not as wonderful as we may have thought ourselves to be. In discovering our dark side, some opportunities for discovery can come from provocative exercises.

By not accepting my shadow, I was sabotaging myself. At work, a colleague who would talk too much in our weekly meetings, take up all the space in the room. I was repressing my own voice to accommodate this inflated personality. As I was making myself small, my resentment would build up. With my shadow work, I had to stay with this resentment and find what was causing this angst. I realized that I needed to find a suitable way to express my own voice. This person had the ability to speak their mind and I was being too timid. I found the courage to discuss this situation with my colleague. Gradually, the weekly forum became a manageable place, not a suffocating one
– Start-up employee, San Francisco

Author Thomas Moore reminds us that a dark night has its own poetic qualities. "It is helpful to constantly broaden your imagination of what is happening to you. If your only idea is that you are depressed, you will be at the mercy of the depression industry, which will treat you as one among millions, for whom there is only one canonical and approved story. Maybe you are overwhelmed and not depressed. Maybe life has sent you a great challenge and you may need a vast spiritual vision to deal with it. To be more of what is capable, to be individual and to be deeply connected is the story of human life."

Within the business world, CEOs wrestle with their own demons, conquering fears, weaknesses and shadows at every turn. One of the Silicon Valley founders had successfully built a company to well over $100 million in revenues. Yet to the chagrin of the investors and the board of directors, the founder would ignore, stall, or deflect any conversations around IPO. Why would a founder stall that grand event that separates the real founders from the also-rans? It was baffling. Several months of attempts later the board gave up but was pleasantly flummoxed when, one fine day, the founder proactively initiated a call to schedule the IPO readiness roadmap. One of the insightful board members discovered that the founder's neighbor had successfully completed her IPO just a few weeks ago. Not to be left behind, this founder overcame his fears of engaging with Wall Street and delivering quarterly earnings. He wanted his IPO too.

Samuel Beckett Accepts His Dark Side

Nobel laureate and author Samuel Beckett's play *Waiting for Godot* is considered to be one of his best creations. While writing this play, he spent most of that year in solitude, only stepping out around midnight to walk among bars in his neighborhood in France. His biographer writes – amid the howling wind churning water, Beckett suddenly realized that the "dark he struggled to keep under" in his life – and in his writing, which had until then failed to find an audience or meet his own aspirations, should, in fact, be the source of his creative inspiration. "I shall always be depressed," Beckett concluded, "but what comforts me is the realization that I can now accept this dark side as the commanding side of my personality. In accepting it, I will make it work for me.

Working with Our Inner Demons

The Tibetan yogi Milarepa welcomes all his demons saying, "It is wonderful you came today. Please come again tomorrow. From time to time, we must converse." While our surface displays the positive, socially acceptable sides such ambition, humor, care and kindness, beneath the surface we all have the repressed dark side, eager to jump out and do some crazy stuff. "Everyone carries a shadow," writes Carl Jung, one of the ardent students of the human shadow. To assume that our dark side is distasteful, dangerous, dirty, or unacceptable is our first misstep. Just as the day and night are inextricably linked, and the two often build upon each other's strengths, so is our shadow. By pretending we have no such thing as a dark side, we are only brushing our psychic dirt under the subconscious carpet, where it remains buried but radioactive. Pulsing to blow up, it manifests in various forms and fears, quirks, and patterns, dragging us by our tail in all directions.

Light is the left hand of darkness and darkness the right hand of light.

Two are one, life and death, lying together like lovers in kemmer,

like hands joined together, like the end and the way.
                                  – Ursula K. Le Guin, The Left Hand of Darkness

---

Jung warns, ". . . the less it is embodied in the individual's conscious life, the blacker and denser it is." When the shadow remains unintegrated, "the conscious becomes the slave of the autonomous shadow," warns Jung. "A man who is possessed by his shadow is always standing in his own light and falling into his own traps . . . living below his own level." In accepting that we have a dark side, we make the first conscious move toward building our awarenesses. Once we accept, we start to welcome and understand the dark side. And finally, we learn to acknowledge it and work with it. Because the price of ignoring it can be severe. If you have read the story of Dr. Jekyll and Mr. Hyde, Jung calls Jekyll, the conscious personality, who fails to integrate his dark side, the evil Mr. Hyde, and succumbs to its machinations.

Inspired by a true event, the tale of Dr. Jekyll and Mr. Hyde highlights the inner fight between the two sides – the good and the bad, the public side and the private side, the light and the dark. Dr. Henry Jekyll represents the respectable public side while the darker Edward Hyde is devoid of a moral compass, beating and killing people. As the story evolves, these two personas battle fiercely to establish dominance. The rational side of Dr. Jekyll starts to consume concoctions and potions to stay within the respectable realm, while his inner demon, his dark side often wrestles control away from him, forcing him to act in a despicable manner. Robert Louis Stevenson got the idea when his friend, Dr. Eugene Chantrelle, was executed for poisoning his wife in his effort to claim a hefty insurance policy. Stevenson attended the court proceedings and was aghast, traumatized as the evidence against Chanterelle unfolded. He would say of Chanterelle, "by all that I could learn of him, he was a model of kindness and good conduct."

As we look at our shadow work, and start to dissect our own psyche, we find opportunities for inquiry along the following:

- *What causes strong reactions, deep fear or admiration? What does this trigger ask of you?*
- *Who do I resent the most? That jerk we encounter at work – what skill or power does he possess?*
- *What traits of theirs cause this resentment? Is it their aggressive style? Their gifted powers of leadership? Their luck or station in life? Their penchant for smooth salesmanship? Their agility and skill in accumulating wealth?*

Thug Life – Facing Your Fears

Bill Plotkin, author of *SoulCraft*, describes his shadow work with recurring dreams of thugs – shadow figures who would threaten, trash, or mug him. "I asked my companions to help me explore the thug of me. I asked if they would be willing to role-play the thugs while I took the part of the victimized and frightened dream-ego." Plotkin gave them the basic scripts and attitudes and asked them to improvise, while he took on the role of a weakling. His eleven companions gladly obliged to thug him around, starting to jab and poke him around. "Things were getting uncomfortable, and uncomfortably real. I began to panic. Tears of sadness and shame spilled from my eyes. And, astonishingly, admiration for the thugs," writes Plotkin.

I realized the thugs of me possessed some qualities I actually admired: a fierce, no-holds-barred genuineness and the ability to look the other guy in the eye and speak the plain truth, regardless of whether it might hurt; their words were from the heart. *The thugs possessed an authenticity, courage, chutzpah, and rough love my ego lacked.* This came as a humbling shock: where I had earlier felt self-righteously victimized, I now felt chagrin for my blindness . . . I exhibited a constraint, a timidity, a social distance that restricted the range and power in my work as a guide as well as in my personal relationships. I vowed to free the slaves of thuggery within me. I adopted the practice of embodying the thug of me, to look people in the eye and speak the plain truth to the best of my ability and with as much love as I could muster. My job was to become that loving thug, to assimilate him. This required emulation of the heart warrior about whom I had spoken for years but had not embodied as much as I might have. I found when I did it skillfully, it worked; people felt seen, honored, deeply met. With few exceptions, they didn't go away feeling mugged, but loved.

As Plotkin shows us, fear often arises from our secret desire to possess some traits or resources ourselves. Put it differently, resentment, like envy, is a form of admiration of attributes we wish we possessed. If you had those skills, position, or resources, would your resentment vanish?

In the deeps are the violence and terror of which psychology has warned us. But if you ride these monsters down if you drop with them farther over the world's rim, you find what our sciences cannot locate or name, the substrate, the ocean or matrix or ether which buoys the rest, which gives goodness its power for good, and evil its power for evil, the unified field: Our complex and inexplicable caring for each other and for our life together here. This is given. It is not learned.

– Annie Dillard

Abandon Notions of Growth, to Allow All Experiences

What does the dark time teach us? How do we use this time to work with our inner demons? To start with, we must surrender to the moment without trying to architect the next phase of our life. "The real task is to live with the darkness, appreciate its unredeemed qualities and appreciate its irreversible value," writes Thomas Moore in *Dark Nights of the Soul*. "You have to give up all notions of growth, success, change, progress and enlightenment. Instead you allow all your experience to have its place. Your job is to be affected by them, letting them do their work for you. You surrender to life . . . not to pain."

And once we surrender to the time, our inner demons can start to tap our shoulders. We become aware of our hidden side, the one that often drives us in subconscious ways. And once we are aware of our demons, we can find ways to integrate them and rebuild our lives. John Moriarty writes, "If nature can handle the destruction and reconstruction of a butterfly, why shouldn't I surrender and trust that it can handle what is happening to me?"

In her book *Your Illustrated Guide to Becoming One with the Universe*, author and artist Yumi Sakugawa says that our inner demons are lonely, desperate to be acknowledged and heard. She suggests that we should welcome them, and have tea and cake with them. And if you face your darkness, "sometimes your demon can give you something in return for your understanding and kindness," she writes.

Next time you feel a pang of envy, take a pause and check in. Ask yourself, what is it exactly that causes this emotional reaction? More often than not, we find that the person we are envious of owns something – an object, a position, or a quality – that subconsciously remains repressed in our desires. In other words, when we see others have something that we have always desired yet been unable to muster up the skills or courage to get, envy sets in. Sustained envy often leads to hostility.

Projecting – What I See in You Lies Dormant in Me

While our repressed parts can build up our dark side, we often project our unfulfilled potential on to other people. Projections can be our own untapped potential, or our own unfulfilled aspirations or unrecognized qualities. Parents start projecting upon their kids rather early, often causing grave damage. Jung solemnly shoved a harsh reality in every parent-child relationship by saying that *the unlived life of the parent is the greatest burden the child must carry.* This is a subject of many therapy sessions, for sure.

What we admire most in others as we grow is present but remains dormant inside us. All that we see – leadership, emotional quotient, grace, ego-mastery, panache, poetic sensitivities, handling wealth with dexterity, and ability to deal with tough mean people. All that is waiting to blossom inside us. The seeds are present and that is what allows you to perceive those very qualities around you. These are stages of projection where every relationship evolves:

- *Ascent* – Admire certain desirable qualities in others, leading to our breathlessness, immense joy, delight. Hero worship, romance, and blind followers subscribe to this stage.
- *Fall* – Realize that they are not really as good as we made them out to be. The emperor has no clothes or my spouse is not as good as I thought she/he would be.

- *Realization* – We may have projected those fantastical qualities upon them ourselves. Our starry-eyed views may be to blame, while they had clay feet all along.
- *Reflection* – What triggers these projections – our needs unfulfilled? Why do we seek such individuals / experiences? What rewards do we receive for our projections along the way? Security? Recognition? Admiration and love?

As founders and CEOs, you might find yourself in excessive admiration of a CEO who has closed a large financing round or hit a solid milestone. In some cases, envy becomes an emotion to contend with. These emotional states are likely your shadow feeling the attraction to what it seeks for you or remorse and envy because you do not have those successful outcomes as yet.

In business, we often find such projections being gladly laid upon our vice president of sales, our board members, venture capitalists (VCs), coaches, mentors, and other figures of adulation. In doing so, we put much pressure on them and do no justice to our own soul.

To establish a level playing field at every juncture, in every relationship is the key to our progress. There is no inferior nor superior – your path is unique in its own way.

25

Prescription 5 – A
Promise to Yourself

Visora González Frontera, a founder based in San Francisco, has suffered from depression, and in managing the highs and lows has struck upon a gentle way of expressing kindness to her own self.

By writing a wonderful letter to her own self.

Talking to your alter ego, a reflection in the pond, can feel strange, even silly. While Narcissus was lost in an admirable gaze of his own beauty, Visora stares at her own reflection and gently brushes away the furrows on that strained brow, caresses the face like a loving mother would. In bringing out such self-compassion, Visora reminds us that there are more ways than one to become self-reliant in our way to recovery.

Visora Frontera shares, "I have often experienced depression, ironically, after a success. When my company received a large innovation grant, I felt 'down' for two solid weeks after hearing the news. I felt shy about discussing my negative feelings with friends because I wanted my 'internal landscape' to reflect the 'external' positive milestone for the company. After reading another founder's account of an enormously successful liquidity event triggering depression, I chose to write. Depressive episodes do not track with a company's balance sheet or an individual's apparent health or well roundedness. Depressive episodes simply happen. I wrote a 'letter to myself' designed to provide believable encouragement (to myself) during 'down' periods. Because depressive feelings generally hamper my ability to hear positive feedback, for me a believable letter must contain the following elements:

1. *Acknowledgment of personal signs/symptoms:* Depression takes many forms yet often has similar outward signs. If you know yours, write them down. You may not experience the same signals every time, but having your own personal list may help you identify depression sooner (and be emboldened to talk about it).

2. *Positive self-talk about core traits:* Entrepreneurs often work for the betterment of the world. We are driven by a desire to improve life for our customers. This remains true whether or not our companies succeed. Because it can be hard to internalize feedback in the midst of perceived difficulty, including positive self-talk which transcends specific situations. Go beyond your current company: write about the traits you most value in yourself. While those traits might feel slightly muted during a depressive episode, those traits definitely still exist. They got you this far and they'll carry you on many future adventures!

3. *Specific, evidence-based feedback:* Research shows that when teachers use generic language to praise students (e.g., 'you did a great job!,' 'you are so good at this!,' etc.), students do not take the feedback seriously. By contrast, when teachers provide behavior-based feedback 'because you took the time to think about that geometry proof and draw your own diagram, I know you have the mathematical maturity to face more difficult math next year'), students take it to heart. Choose specific examples to illustrate the core traits you identified. Providing a mountain of evidence about positive prior events may help the self-judgment machine take a break.

4. *Reminder to feel your feelings:* This letter is not meant to curtail the depressive episode. Different individuals manage depression differently. You likely have specific resources which help you manage depression (examples include aerobic exercise, playing music, therapy,

antidepressant medication, making art, meditating, phoning a friend, spending time in a religious community, etc.). Include those ideas in your letter while also noting that it can take time to 'feel normal' again."

This letter is not meant to stop the depression in its tracks: it is meant to serve as a reminder that you will get through this.

Dear Self:

I choose to live the often-uncertain life of an entrepreneur in pursuit of the creation of new technologies representing my deepest values. I write this letter now – a "letter to myself" – as a point of reference I can turn to when I come face-to-face with self-doubt or depression, two psychological wraiths I often find at my side in times of great challenge. Self-doubt and depression can cause me to forget to eat proper meals, forsake my hobbies ("I'll get back to playing music next week"), ignore social invitations, experience less pleasure during favorite activities, focus only on the "hardest" tasks at work, and feel tired even after a solid night's sleep.

I used to wish a magical enlightened being would materialize to validate the life choices I have made over the years in support of my start-up companies. I wanted my own personal council of mythical elders to nod at me at the end of each workday as I shut down my computer, white-haired wise creatures smiling quietly to themselves and remarking, "Look at this one: writing code, wrangling clients, and managing engineers day after day. How marvelous!" When I encounter depression, I tend to ignore all positive feedback I receive from mere mortals. Self-judgment hampers my ability to see start-up life as a balance between intense struggle and intense joy. I forget why I chose entrepreneurship to begin with – I lose sight of the bright spots in my personal grand vision for society.

Life might feel easier without a grand vision. I might wake up in the morning unperturbed by the injustices around me. Dulling myself to the pains of the world, perhaps I could

236 PRESCRIPTION 5 – A PROMISE TO YOURSELF

retreat into a placid existence devoid of self-judgment and devoid of sadness.

But that existence lacks one essential ingredient: shadow. Injustice depresses me because I dare to experience thoughtfulness in a world in which carelessness too often rules the day. I live with a bold curiosity that drives me to ask hard questions and pursue never-before-tried ideas. Every time I experience shadows, I learn more about the problems I wish to solve. When I choose to learn a new skill, I often continue until I have the capacity to teach that skill to others. I hold myself to exacting standards because I want to discover the road on which I will contribute to the best of my ability and in a way that is uniquely mine.

Let this letter remind me that I have already found that road. I found it when I taught precalculus to a deaf student during high school. I found it laughing when a friend and I built a recumbent bicycle neither one of us could control. I found it studying linear algebra on my own at night, building a chicken coop for a neighbor, stripping down to my underwear to excavate a snow cave large enough to sleep in, teaching Python to librarians, and quitting my corporate job to take a risk starting a company in the energy sector. This is me: a self-starter, a partner, an impassioned learner, a point in a constellation of community, a spontaneous musician, an adventurer, and more things yet to come.

I have an irrepressible will to use my technical skills to advance equity in the world today, furthering the work of Dr. Martin Luther King Jr. and other civil rights leaders. Whether or not my projects succeed, and whether or not the world feels dark, I would rather labor under a grand vision than dodge my responsibilities as an innovator and leader.

Eunice Kennedy Shriver said it best in creating the motto for the Special Olympics:

"Let me win."

"But if I cannot win, let me be brave in the attempt."

On the road,

Visora González Frontera

Visora's letter is a simple and soulful example of self-care in the journey of entrepreneurship. And reminds us:

If we cannot win, let us be brave in the attempt.

26

The Elements of a Good Life

When it is all done, how do we know it was a life well lived, that the pain was all worth it?

What should we look back on? As we know, entrepreneurs have accepted Joseph Schumpeter as their God, and have a raging desire to disrupt the status quo. Propelled to deliver magical gifts to society, the founder's journey is beset with dreams of largesse. Electricity, rocket ships, autonomous vehicles, flying cars, a GPT-3 based intelligent world where our brains are transcranially linked to search engines. Nothing is impossible.

To pull such magical feats, it is necessary for founders to have cognitive dissonance, a ravenously high appetite for risk, a false perception of their own invincibility, superpowers and magical sleights of hand, not fazed by the stigma of failure. What is failure anyway? After all, that's just a point of view. Such mantras allow founders to be special in their own way. But for some, this causes a unique form of madness; their mercurial minds can turn against themselves. What silent force gives tenacity and fortitude to some, and fatigues others – we will never fully understand nor know?

A life well lived is exemplified by a series of longitudinal studies conducted by Harvard Medical School researchers. Over 800 people agreed to share facets of their lives and stayed engaged in the study from their teens to old age. The goal – to identify traits and characteristics that led to a fulfilling life.

In *Aging Well: Surprising Guideposts to a Happier Life* from the Landmark Harvard Study of Adult Development, author George Vaillant describes some individual histories and identifies six factors that contributed to graceful and satisfying old age. I have simplified some of these:

1. *Development of own self and an integrated identity –*
   - How has your own thinking, perspectives, passions, and values developed independent from your parents and social influences?
   - Do you believe you have the ability to master the demands of modern life?

2. *Ability to form and grow intimate relationships –*
   - How have you emotionally evolved to form intimate, reciprocal, and committed relationships? Note that these relationships are not necessarily with a spouse or a sexual partner, but with a wider group of individuals across a diverse backdrop.

3. *The progression of your career*
   - In the four aspects of your career, how do you rate your own self?
     - Competence – Do you believe you have the skills to contribute to your work?
     - Commitment – Are you bringing your time, energy, and intensity to your work to make a difference?
     - Compensation – Are you taking a fair compensation that allows you to live a comfortable lifestyle? Most start-up founders struggle on this front.
     - Contentment – Considering everything you do, do you feel a sense of satisfaction, comfort, and possibly a sense of accomplishment?
   - *Is your identity separate from your work? How will people see your life beyond your career?*

4. *Ability to give to others – your role in community*
   - How do you support the autonomy of the next generation, without forcing your rigid and outdated views?
   - What values do you preserve and carry forward, and which ones do you let go?
   - In what way do you help build communities – especially where you do not gain any financial rewards?

5. *Integrity of one's life*
   - When you look back at life, do you accept the rewards without regrets? Or are you overwhelmed by losses, sadness, or grief?
   - In your final years, how will you close the books and let go of all attachments gradually, and peacefully?

The sum of my life is no more than three words
I was raw
I was cooked
I was burnt

— Twelfth-century Persian poet Rumi,
alluding to the stages of life

Desiderata – Max Ehrmann

Go placidly amid the noise and the haste, and remember what peace there may be in silence.

As far as possible, without surrender, be on good terms with all persons.

Speak your truth quietly and clearly; and listen to others, even to the dull and the ignorant; they too have their story.

Avoid loud and aggressive persons; they are vexatious to the spirit. If you compare yourself with others, you may become vain or bitter, for always there will be greater and lesser persons than yourself.

Enjoy your achievements as well as your plans. Keep interested in your own career, however humble; it is a real possession in the changing fortunes of time.

Exercise caution in your business affairs, for the world is full of trickery. But let this not blind you to what virtue there is; many persons strive for high ideals, and everywhere life is full of heroism.

Be yourself. Especially do not feign affection. Neither be cynical about love; for in the face of all aridity and disenchantment, it is as perennial as the grass.

Take kindly the counsel of the years, gracefully surrendering the things of youth.

Nurture strength of spirit to shield you in sudden misfortune. But do not distress yourself with dark imaginings. Many fears are born of fatigue and loneliness.

Beyond a wholesome discipline, be gentle with yourself. You are a child of the universe no less than the trees and the stars; you have a right to be here.

And whether or not it is clear to you, no doubt the universe is unfolding as it should. Therefore be at peace with God, whatever you conceive Him to be. And whatever your labors and aspirations, in the noisy confusion of life, keep peace in your soul.

With all its sham, drudgery, and broken dreams, it is still a beautiful world.

Be cheerful. Strive to be happy.

Postscript: How to Care for the Broken and the Depressed

> *It would be easier for me to discuss my mental health issues if it was not such a charged topic . . . if my friends did not try to address my depression themselves.*
>
> — Founder, United States

> *Researchers believe that the inability of the depressed to respond to offers of help is one of the most aversive qualities of depression. Just as workers will not end a strike until their employer offers a significant increase in salary, most initial offers of help do not lead to recovery from depression. The depressed have serious problems and the initial offers of help are "too small" to solve them. The depressed need to compel substantially better offers from reluctant social partners.*
>
> — Edward Hagen and Kristen Syme, University of Washington[1]

In the past we locked the depressed up in distant places like hospitals and sanitariums. We even used electric shocks. We hide them, ignore them, or make them go away. Maybe because we are not equipped to talk about these topics.

At home, we try to fix the problem ourselves. We rush in to help friends and family members but have no tools.

Our fear, helplessness, and panic set in. Our own discomfort creates a bigger problem. We try to avoid both – our discomfort as well as the depressed person. As we are unable to handle our own inner states, we run away from the ones who are depressed. We have neither the right language nor the tools, but this is a start.

TOP REASONS FOUNDERS DO NOT ASK

Social media is rife with tweets about reaching out and asking for help. But we don't really want to talk about it. Fear of judgment and stigma is real. And most people cannot handle it or are poor listeners.

Yashar Ali @yashar · Jun 6

1. Sharing as much as I have about this episode and passive suicidal ideation as it's happening has made me even more empathetic when it comes to mental health stigmas.

The number of people making assumptions about what triggered this is shocking but not surprising

96   135   3.4K

Yashar Ali @yashar · Jun 6

2. The number of people who offer unhelpful unsolicited advice...shocking but not surprising.

The number of people who make aggressive demands about what I should/shouldn't be doing...shocking but not surprising.

A reminder of why people don't talk about mental health issues.

179   143   3.8K

Researchers state that depressed people have a distinctive style of communication that is effective at expressing sadness and despair but not other emotions. Their conversations signal that they have problems. They want to talk about them and gain reassurance and support.[2]

Founders struggling with depression shared the top reasons they do not reach out or ask for help:

Fear and Repercussions

- *Fear of judgment and stigma. "I feel broken," writes one founder.*
- *Fear and shame of being perceived as weak or incapable ... admission of failure. My investors did not take me seriously when I tried to share my mental health challenges. As a society, we are obsessed with proving how strong we are and with outlandish displays of strength. There are times when I don't think I can handle the pressure.*
- *Fear of being marginalized at work. "Speaking about this at work or discussing this with investors is a career-limiting move."*
- *Fear of being taken advantage of.*
- *Fear of scaring people away, or losing respect.*

Sympathy and Pity

- *I don't want pity or false assurances.*
- *I don't want people to treat me differently.*
- *As female CEOs, we are often stereotyped as being weak. I cannot feed this stereotype by sharing my condition.*

Sense of Responsibility

- *I should not be dumping on or spreading my gloom/making others sad with my baggage.*
- *People don't want to hear your negative stuff and want to be around positive people so I mostly keep quiet.*
- *The last person anyone is worried about is the CEO. It is really lonely in my role.*

WHAT DO THE DEPRESSED NEED?

"I just need someone to hold my hand and say some simple comforting words like 'I too would feel stressed – I know building a company is scary,'" writes one founder. Another founder said that empathy comes from knowing the pain. "The only people who seem to understand are the ones who have been through it, which is why we have built a small CEO support group." But not everyone may have the luxury of having like-minded CEOs in their network or region.

Founders tell us what they need:

- *We need the same friendships and support and care, just like any other human being.*
- *Simple and "mild" check-ins. A call or text to see how I'm doing. A walk in the evening or a meal.*
- *Safe environments - authentic/honest engagement – no judgments or extreme reactions, without trying to solve my problems. **Also, don't give advice. Just empathize.***
- *Listening nonjudgmentally, be comfortable in silence, hold the space, and give me space if I need it.*

- *Just love me as I am. Let me know that I'm loved. No need for you to try and be perfect in your effort.*
- *Get educated on depression. We don't even have a vocabulary for how to deal with sadness, or how to act when others around us are sad. How can we teach this to our children?*

WHEN YOU MEET SOMEONE
DEEP IN GRIEF

Slip off your needs
and set them by the door.

Enter barefoot
this darkened chapel

hollowed by loss
hallowed by sorrow

its gray stone walls
and floor.

You, congregation
of one

are here to listen
not to sing.

Kneel in the back pew.
Make no sound,

let the candles
speak.

Patricia McKernon Runkle

On a rare occasion, when we have an opportunity to help others or offer advice, it can be extremely seductive. We feel important. We often gladly give advice without fully appreciating the fact that we may not be qualified to do so, or our that perspectives may be colored or flawed in their own way. Each one may have different thresholds of motivation, confidence, willpower, and perseverance.

You have to help another person. But it's not right to play God with masses of people. To be God you have to know what you're doing. And to do any good at all, just believing you're right and your motives are good isn't enough.
— *Ursula K. Le Guin,* The Lathe of Heaven

WHAT THE DEPRESSED DO NOT NEED

Founders unequivocally share what they do NOT need:

- Stop cheering me on. Saying stuff like "You are a star and you will shine" – it only worsens my mood and adds pressure.
- Don't try to get me out of my mood. I cannot turn off sad feelings – there is no kill switch. I did not hire you as my cheerleader, did I?
- Once you know about it, let me be the one to bring up the topic and anything about my mental health and depression. I don't want advice, just acknowledgment.
- Try not to start our conversation every time with "So how have you been feeling?" or say things like "You can do it" or "Keep trying – you will get out of it." Many try to build me up as a "can-do" hero, which does not help.
- I am not looking for any special treatment. My being depressed doesn't mean I am unable to have a normal conversation about weather, funny incidents, and life in general.
- Don't tell me your own stories: I know you may be trying to empathize by saying it happens to everyone but stop telling me your own stories and hijacking the

conversation. I am trying to express my feelings and you jumping in with your own stories is being insensitive or even incredibly unaware and selfish.

- Curb your discomfort, anger, and sarcasm:. "When my partner made a joke out of it when I shared my mental health challenges, I knew I had to ask for help elsewhere. This made me even more sad," writes one founder. My spouse jumps at me, screaming, "Are you depressed again?" when I am having a bad day. They are afraid or worried that I might become a bigger liability for them.

- No advice or unsolicited inquiries.

HOW TO HELP – A FEW GOOD EXAMPLES

Some deeply touching ways to respectfully support someone as they go through this journey can be seen from these examples.

Carl Jung, in a letter to a friend, warns against half-hearted measures:

> *Dear N.,*
>
> *I am sorry you are so miserable. "Depression" means literally "being forced downwards." This can happen even when you don't consciously have any feeling at all of being "on top"! So I wouldn't dismiss this hypothesis out of hand. If I had to live in a foreign country, I would seek out one or two people who seemed amiable and would make myself useful to them, so that libido came to me from outside, even though in a somewhat primitive form, say of a dog wagging its tail.*
>
> *I would turn in rage against myself and with the heat of my rage I would melt my lead. I would renounce everything and engage in the lowest activities should my depression drive me to violence. I would wrestle with the dark angel until he dislocated my hip. For he is also the light and the blue sky which he withholds from me.*
>
> *Anyway that is what I would do. What others would do is another question, which I cannot answer. But for you too there is an instinct either to back out of it or to go down to the depths. But no half-measures or half-heartedness.*

In this letter, Jung points out the importance of seeking a few people out, maybe moving to another country – a change of scenery. But the inner work required to acknowledge that the dark angel is also the light and the blue sky, which depression withholds – these are sheer gems of wisdom. Whatever we do, Jung says, do it with every fiber of our soul.

In another example, singer and songwriter Jewel wrote a letter to Tony Hsieh, CEO of Zappos, in which she prescribes the company of right people. "I am going to be blunt, I need to tell you that I don't think you are well and in your right mind. I think you are taking too many drugs that cause you to disassociate ... The people you are surrounding yourself with are either ignorant or willing to be complicit in you killing yourself."

If I had a friend and loved him because of the benefits which this brought me and because of getting my own way, then it would not be my friend that I loved but myself. I should love my friend on account of his own goodness and virtues and on account of all that he is in himself. Only if I love my friend in this way do I love him properly.

– Meister Eckhart

It's Only Darkness, Not the End

Author Henry James shares his own helplessness as he offers authentic advice to friend and author Grace Norton. Henry, who had his own bouts of depression, avoids offering precise solutions to Grace. As we read his letter, his compassion and deep wisdom shine through.

My dear Grace,

Before the sufferings of others I am always utterly powerless, and the letter you gave me reveals such depths of suffering that I hardly know what to say to you. This indeed is not my last word – but it must be my first. You are not isolated, verily, in such states of feeling as this – that is, in the sense that you appear to make all the misery of all mankind your own; only I have a terrible sense that you give all and receive nothing – that there is no reciprocity in your sympathy – that you have all the affliction of it and none of the returns. However – I am determined not to speak to you except with the voice of stoicism.

I don't know why we live – the gift of life comes to us from I don't know what source or for what purpose; but I believe we can go on living for the reason that (always of course up to a certain point) life is the most valuable thing we know anything about and it is therefore presumptively a great mistake to surrender it while there is any yet left in the cup. In other words consciousness is an illimitable power, and though at times it may seem to be all consciousness of misery, yet in the way it propagates itself from wave to wave, so that we never cease to feel, though at moments we appear to, try to, pray to, there is something that holds one in one's place, makes it a standpoint in the universe which it is probably good not to forsake. You are right in your consciousness that we are all echoes and reverberations of the same, and you are noble when your interest and pity as to everything that surrounds you, appears to have a sustaining and harmonizing power. Only don't, I beseech you, generalize too much in these sympathies and tendernesses – remember that every life is a special problem which is not yours but another's, and content yourself with the terrible algebra of your own. Don't melt too much into the universe, but be as solid and dense and fixed as you can. We all live together, and those of us who love and know, live so most. We help each other – even unconsciously, each in our own effort, we lighten the effort of others, we contribute to the sum of success, make it possible for others to live. Sorrow comes in great waves – no one can know that better than you – but it rolls over us, and though it may almost smother us it leaves us on the spot and we know that if it is strong we are stronger, inasmuch as it passes and we remain. It wears us, uses us, but we wear it and use it in return; and it is blind, whereas we after a manner see.

My dear Grace, you are passing through a darkness in which I myself in my ignorance see nothing but that you have been made wretchedly ill by it; but it is only a darkness, it is not an end, or the end. Don't think, don't feel, any more than you can help, don't conclude or decide—don't do anything but wait. Everything will pass, and serenity and accepted mysteries and disillusionments, and the tenderness of a few good people, and new opportunities and ever so much of life, in a word, will remain. You will do all sorts of things yet, and I will help you. The only thing is not to melt in the meanwhile. I insist upon the necessity of a sort of mechanical condensation – so that however fast the horse may run away there will, when he pulls up, be a somewhat agitated but perfectly identical G. N. left in the saddle. Try not to be ill – that is all; for in that there is a future. You are marked out for success, and you must not fail. You have my tenderest affection and all my confidence.

Ever your faithful friend—
Henry James,
July 1883

Reading Poetry Aloud

In previous sections of this book, we covered the joy of reading poetry, possibly to help our own selves. But reading poetry to a friend who may be down can be therapeutic, calming, and caring in so many ways. Before you head over with a fat volume of Whitman, Rupi Kaur, or Emily Dickinson, do make sure that poetry is their thing – that they care about and like poems – else you run the risk of exacerbating their pain, all the while thinking you are really helping them.

In this touching example of caring for the broken, Phillip Moffitt, former president of *Esquire* magazine, writes about David, his dear friend who stood by him in his darkest hour. When Phillip sold the publishing company, he went through a deeply troubling time – call it depression, or being lost in the woods. In such moments of despair, one of his friends flew to New York and spent the weekend with Phillip. "When I was struggling with my emotional chaos, David flew to New York and spent a weekend reading T.S. Eliot's "Little Gidding" from *Four Quartets* out loud to me. It was the first time I realized the deep wisdom with which Eliot addressed the modern dilemma of suffering, and Eliot's words continued to be of great comfort to me during that difficult period."

Wait, what? Two men. Reading poetry. Out loud! WTF are these dudes doing?

But once we look beneath the surface, "Little Gidding" is a pretty amazing poem.

The poem is *very* long (no wonder it took a whole weekend to read it) but touches, in very subtle ways, *how time heals everything, how all shall be well, and how patience is key.*

And that the fires within purify us so that we can become like a rose.

Reading poems to strangers as they walk by – San Francisco

Let's Make Stories Together

When a founder's close friend was struggling with depression, she used a gentle yet creative way to help him through the dark nights:

My friend was in a pretty bad place, had lost all hope, was down, wiped out, and completely distraught. I was out of options on how to help him when I found this ray of hope. In one of our conversations, I recalled his love of reading fiction and short stories.

One such story – it was our favorite – was The Phantom of the Opera. Later that night, I hatched up a plan and called him the next day. I told my friend that we should read the book again together, with the intention of writing its sequel. At first, it was hard, almost impossible to get him to read this book again but I stuck with this crazy idea.

I called him each day. Soon he dragged himself to reading the book again. Within a few weeks, we had started to discuss the characters, their motives, and the plot. It was several months later that this story's sequel became a reason for our ongoing conversations.

In my role, all I did was create a room for creative possibilities in his life. We were soon into the thick of a detailed plot for the sequel, complete with multiple storylines, character development, and a cliff-hanger ending. I almost wept with joy when one day, I heard him say, "After this sequel, can we write the third part?" I knew we had started to make progress.

Massaging the Soles of Your Feet

And then there is the mother of all examples – unheard of and unparalleled in its level of care: massaging the feet of a depressed friend.

Parker Palmer, an author and educator who was supported by his friend amidst his depression writes,

There was this one friend who came to me, after asking permission to do so, every afternoon about four o'clock, sat me down in a chair in the living room, took off my shoes and socks, and massaged my feet. He hardly ever said anything. He was a Quaker elder. And yet out of his intuitive sense, from time to time would say a very brief word like, "I can feel your struggle today," or farther down the road, "I feel that you're a little stronger at this moment, and I'm glad for that." But beyond that, he would say hardly anything. He would give no advice. He would simply report from time to time what he was sort of intuiting about my condition.

Somehow he found the one place in my body, namely, the soles of my feet, where I could experience some sort of connection to another human being. And the act of massaging just, you know, in a way that I really don't have words for, kept me connected with the human race.

What he mainly did for me, of course, was to be willing to be present to me in my suffering. He just hung in with me in this very quiet, very simple, very tactile way. And I've never really been able to find the words to fully express my gratitude for that, but I know it made a huge difference. And it became for me a metaphor of the kind of community we need to extend to people who are suffering in this way, which is a community that is neither invasive of the mystery nor evasive of the suffering but is willing to hold people in a space, a sacred space of relationship, where somehow this person who is on the dark side of the moon can get a little confidence that they can come around to the other side.

In hearing such narratives, we have to admire the sensitivity, awareness, and bonds that exist between such friends – where one of them knows the other well enough to offer – feels comfortable massaging the soles of the other's feet – and the other is equally comfortable receiving this gift with grace.

It takes two to tango. The receiver as well as the giver must dance to the same beat. If you don't know someone really well, showing up at their door and offering to massage their feet may positively spook them out.

Good intentions have to be anchored and centered around their needs, not what we want to do to feel good about ourselves.

Approach the Depressed with Care

Approach the depressed as you would approach a wounded animal, a deer or a gentle rabbit, hiding in the forest, trying to recuperate. Approach very slowly. Build trust.

And let them show where the wounds are. To care for the depressed is not easy – for they are hiding in their shell most of the time.

In building the core of trust with another, we can write our own code of conduct:

1. Reliable – I am reliable and I am here when you need to speak with me.
2. Steady – Your situation does not cause me to panic or be afraid. It invokes the caring side of me.
3. Support and Servitude – I am here to serve. This is about what you need, not what I think you should do. I have no agenda but to make sure you become resilient.
4. Responsibility – I know the limits of what I can do and what I cannot do. I know when we may need to ask for professional help. I am not trying to be your one-stop shop, monopoly emotional store, nor am I playing God, but being a companion.
5. Trust – I do not judge you, discuss your situation with anyone, criticize, or gossip.
6. Detachment – I do not have preconceived notions of your progress, recovery, or outcomes. I am here to have a conversation and just be by your side. If you do not reciprocate, I will have no hard feelings.

"You must be very patient," said the Fox.

"First you will sit down at a little distance from me in the grass.

I shall look at you out of the corner of my eye, and you will say nothing.

Words are the source of misunderstandings.

But you will sit a little closer to me, every day

    – From *The Little Prince* by Antoine de Saint-Exupéry

Basket Of Figs

-by Ellen Bass

Bring me your pain, love. Spread
it out like fine rugs, silk sashes,
warm eggs, cinnamon
and cloves in burlap sacks. Show me
the detail, the intricate embroidery
on the collar, tiny shell buttons,
the hem stitched the way you were taught,
pricking just a thread, almost invisible.
Unclasp it like jewels, the gold
still hot from your body. Empty
your basket of figs. Spill your wine.
That hard nugget of pain, I would suck it,
cradling it on my tongue like the slick
seed of pomegranate. I would lift it
tenderly, as a great animal might
carry a small one in the private
cave of the mouth

Appendix I: A Founder's Mental Health Manifesto

Several founders described their start-up challenges, where they felt trapped, or wanted to pursue one idea after another. It is like a drug, just of a different kind. The brain is indeed addicted to being in the "hunt" mode as opposed to rested, relaxed and relishing modes. Spinning in the labyrinth, or like Sisyphus rolling stones uphill, these founders were exhausted and sought relief, a desire to break free from the machine.

As Jerry Colonna often asks, "When do you know it's enough?" We fail to find a state of contentment and are always hunting for our next kill. One of the beleaguered founders suggested that we should build a mental health manifesto, and even seek a community support model.

In this rough cut of a manifesto, built upon the time-tested AA program, I hope entrepreneurs would be able to brave their way out of the dark nights.

1. Acceptance – We admit we were powerless over the force of depression – that our lives themselves had become unmanageable and disrupted.

2. Belief – We have come to believe that we cannot restore our own selves to a normal way of thinking and living.

3. Letting go – We have made a decision to turn our will and our lives over to the care of a suitable power of our own understanding, be it therapists, coaches, or trusted and capable friends.

4. Self-reflection – We have made a searching and fear-less inventory of ourselves and our weaknesses as entrepreneurs.

5. Self-admission – We have admitted to ourselves and to another human being the exact nature of our challenges, shortcomings, and wrongs.

6. Ready for change – We are entirely ready to grow, to have any defects removed, and we are ready for change.

7. Asking for help – We have humbly invoked the intention and expressed the desire to help remove our shortcomings.

8. Forgiveness, if needed – We have made lists of all persons we had harmed and became willing to make amends to them all.

9. Direct efforts – We make direct efforts to work with our shortcomings, and make amends with such people wherever possible, except when to do so would injure them or others.

10. Ongoing efforts – We have continued to take personal inventory, and when we veered off and were wrong, we promptly admitted it.

11. Serving others through our life – We have sought to improve our conscious contact with higher power, be it the mysterious force of Life, Higher Purpose, Spirit, Society, or God as we understand it, praying only for knowledge of Life's plan and will for us and the power to carry that out.

12. Support other entrepreneurs – We have made an effort to practice these principles in all our affairs, so we can carry this message to other struggling entrepreneurs and tribe members so that they too can benefit from our experiences.

Appendix II: Founders' Voices and Anonymized Surveys

As this book was being conceived, Brad Feld and I reached out to the founder community and asked for their anonymized inputs. We created a questionnaire of about 15 open-ended questions.

Over 150 founders from across the world responded. They shared their insights, perspectives, and challenges on mental health. All the voices have been included in the book, and some have been edited for clarity or space. Because the survey was anonymized, we believe it lends authenticity to their voices.

Aaron Swartz once said that there is still an enormous stigma in being sick, and we fully understand this social conundrum. Of course, there are several shortcomings in this survey methodology. For one, it's a snapshot in time, and also, it was pre-Covid. I am sure, for some, the founders' challenges were even more exacerbated amidst the pandemic.

Coincidentally, I came across the work done by Jan Chipchase and Jonny Miller. They had recently completed a survey – "Emotional Resilience in Leadership Report," October 2020 – in which they gathered 261 respondents from 43 countries, and followed up with 26 follow-up phone interviews. I am grateful to them for sharing their findings. The duo operate a virtual masterclass exploring resilience fundamentals, through integrating resilience practices into your day, combining in-depth talks, hands-on activities, and group explorations. For more details see https://studiodradiodurans.com/products/emotional-resillience-masterclass.

A longitudinal study would be an excellent opportunity to better understand how founders' mental conditions evolve with external factors. And finally, the responses were partially subjective – data is neither empirical nor longitudinal. There are no statistical variances, ML models, inferences, hypotheses, or p values we had to calculate, thank God!

Notes

Introduction: The Despondent Founder

1. The words *founder*, *CEO*, and *entrepreneur* are used interchangeably across this book.
2. Matthew Cooper, "I'm Stepping Down as CEO Due to My Mental Health—and I Want to Talk About It," *Quartz*, December 18, 2020, https://qz.com/work/1947585/earnups-matthew-cooper-im-leaving-as-ceo-due-to-mental-health/.

Chapter 1: When Suicide Seems Like a Good Option

1. K. L. Syme, Z. H. Garfield, and E. H. Hagen, "Testing the Bargaining vs. Inclusive Fitness Models of Suicidal Behavior against the Ethnographic Record," *Evolution and Human Behavior* 37, no. 3 (2016): 179–192.
2. Repeated thoughts and excessive ruminations are a cry for help.
3. J. Kruger and D. Dunning, "Unskilled and Unaware of It: How Difficulties in Recognizing One's Own Incompetence Lead to Inflated Self-Assessments," *Journal of Personality and Social Psychology* 77, no. 6 (1999): 1121–1134. https://doi.org/10.1037/0022-3514.77.6.1121

Chapter 2: Stepping Back from the Edge

1. M. ten Have, B. W. J. H. Penninx, M. Tuithof, S. van Dorsselaer, M. Kleinjan, J. Spijker, and R. de Graaf, "Duration of Major and Minor Depressive Episodes and Associated Risk Indicators in a Psychiatric Epidemiological Cohort Study of the General Population," *Acta Psychiatrica Scandinavica*, May 16, 2017, https://doi.org/10.1111/acps.12753

Chapter 3: How External Events Trigger Negative Feelings

1. K. S. Kendler, L. M. Karkowski, and C. A. Prescott, "Causal Relationship Between Stressful Life Events and the Onset of Major Depression," *American Journal of Psychiatry* 156, no. 6 (1999): 837.
2. Ryan Caldbeck, "Transitions," October 15, 2020, https://ryancaldbeck.medium.com/transitions-fa7ce4af435.
3. Dr. Lucy Hone, "The Three Secrets of Resilient People," TEDXChristchurch, September 25, 2019, https://www.youtube.com/watch?v=NWH8N-BvhAw.

Chapter 5: Building Our Psychological Quotient

1. Jill Lepore, "It's Just Too Much: Has Burnout Become the Human Condition?" *The New Yorker*, May 24, 2021.

Chapter 8: Ego – The Emperor and the Slave

1. From Richard Boothby, *Sex on the Couch: What Freud Still Has to Teach Us About Sex and Gender* (New York: Routledge, 2014).
2. From Adam Phillips, *On Balance* (New York: Farrar, Straus and Giroux, 2010).

Chapter 10: The Hidden Land of Desires and Motivations

1. Arthur C. Clarke in Andrew Chaikin, "Meeting of the Minds: Buzz Aldrin Visits Arthur C. Clarke," *Space Illustrated*, February 27, 2001.

Chapter 14: Toward Building a Healthy Ego

1. J. Miller and J. Chipchase, "Emotional Resilience in Leadership Report," 2020.

Chapter 19: Medicating Our Way to Recovery

1. K. S. Kendler, "Toward a Philosophical Structure for Psychiatry," *American Journal of Psychiatry* 162, no. 3 (2005): 433–440.

2. E. H. Hagen, "Evolutionary Theories of Depression: A Critical Review," *Canadian Journal of Psychiatry* 56, no. 12 (2011): 716–726.

3. From Brihadaranyaka Upanishad, adapted from Madhu Kanda, Chapter II.

4. J. Naumann, J. Grebe, S. Kaifel, T. Weinert, C. Sadahiani, and R. Huber, "Effects of Hyperthermic Baths on Depression, Sleep and Heart Rate Variability in Patients with Depressive Disorder: A Randomized Clinical Pilot Trial," *BMC Complementary and Alternative Medicine* 17, no. 1 (2017): 172.

5. S. Stretton, "Systematic Review on the Primary and Secondary Reporting of the Prevalence of Ghostwriting in the Medical Literature," *BMJ Open* 4, no. 7 (2014): e004777.

6. E. H. Turner, A. M. Matthews, E. Linardatos, R. A. Tell, and R. Rosenthal, "Selective Publication of Antidepressant Trials and Its Influence on Apparent Efficacy," *New England Journal of Medicine* 358, no. 3 (2008): 252–260.

7. J. Kaiser, "Senate Probe of Research Psychiatrists," *Science* 325, no. 5936 (2009): 30; M. Perrone, "Glaxo Used Ghostwriting to Promote Paxil: Offered to Help Doctors Publish Articles on Drugs," Associated Press/*Boston Globe* [online edition], August 20, 2009, News Section; D. Wilson, "Drug Maker Hired a Writing Company for Doctors' Book, Documents Say," *New York Times* [online edition], November 29, 2010, Business Day Section.

8. D. Healy and M. Thase, "Is Academic Psychiatry for Sale?," *British Journal of Psychiatry* 182, no. 5 (2003): 1–3.

9. Michael Mezher, "Company Challenges UK Clinical Trial Transparency Rules," *Regulatory Focus*, May 18, 2015, https://www.raps.org/regulatory-focus%e2%84%a2/news-articles/2015/5/company-challenges-uk-clinical-trial-transparency-rules.

10. D. A. Regier, C. T. Kaelber, D. S. Rae, M. E. Farmer, B. Knauper, R. C. Kessler, and G. S. Norquist, "Limitations of Diagnostic Criteria and Assessment Instruments for Mental Disorders: Implications for Research and Policy," *Archives of General Psychiatry* 55, no. 2 (1998): 109–115; R. L. Spitzerand J. C. Wakefield, "DSM-IV Diagnostic Criterion for Clinical Significance: Does It Help Solve the False Positives Problem?" *American Journal of Psychiatry* 156, no. 12 (1999): 1856–1864.

11. I. Kirsch, T. J. Moore, A. Scoboria, and S. S. Nicholls, "The Emperor's New Drugs: An Analysis of Antidepressant Medication Data Submitted to the U.S. Food and Drug Administration," *Prevention & Treatment* 5, no. 1 (2002): 23; I. Kirsch, B. J. Deacon, T. B. Huedo-Medina, A. Scoboria, T. J. Moore, and B. T. Johnson, "Initial Severity and Antidepressant Benefits: A Meta-analysis of Data Submitted to the Food and Drug Administration," *PLoS Medicine* 5, no. 2 (2008): e45; J. C. Fournier, R. J. DeRubeis, S. D. Hollon, S. Dimidjian, J. D. Amsterdam, R. C. Shelton, and J. Fawcett, "Antidepressant Drug Effects and Depression Severity: A Patient-level Meta-analysis." *JAMA* 303, no. 1 (2010): 47–53.

12. J. W. Williams, C. D. Mulrow, E. Chiquette, P. H. Noël, C. Aguilar, and J. Cornell, "A Systematic Review of Newer Pharmacotherapies for Depression in Adults: Evidence Report Summary," *Annals of Internal Medicine* 132, no. 9 (2000): 743–756.

Chapter 20: A Soul Made Cheerful

1. Ryan Caldbeck, "Transitions," October 15, 2020, https:// ryancaldbeck.medium.com/transitions-fa7ce4af435

Chapter 21: Prescription 1 – An Organized Diminution of Work

1. Ryan Caldbeck, "Transitions," October 5, 2020, https:// ryancaldbeck.medium.com/transitions-fa7ce4af435

Chapter 22: Prescription 2 – Get Out of Your Head

1. M. R. Marselle, D. E. Bowler, J. Watzema, D. Eichenberg, T. Kirsten, and A. Bonn, "Urban Street Tree Biodiversity and Antidepressant Prescriptions," *Scientific Reports* 10, 22445 (2020), https://doi.org/10.1038/s41598-020-79924-5.

Postscript: How to Care for the Broken and the Depressed

1. E. H. Hagen and K. L. Syme, "Credible Sadness, Coercive Sadness: Depression as a Functional Response to Adversity and Strife," *Oxford Handbook of Evolution and the Emotions* (L. Al-Shawaf and T. Shackelford, Eds.).
2. Ibid.

About the Author

Mahendra Ramsinghani is a San Francisco–based venture investor focused on early-stage high-technology companies. Over the past decade, he has invested in over a hundred technology start-ups. He has authored two leading books on venture capital and startups: *The Business of Venture Capital* (Wiley Finance, 2021) and *Startup Boards* (Wiley, 2014) co-authored with noted author and investor Brad Feld.

This book came from the realization that managing investor relationships and board dynamics is easy compared to managing our own internal struggles. Amidst the pandemic, these struggles were heightened. To offer a voice to these struggles, and to catalog and curate the mind maps (and to possibly soothe his own madness), he wrote this book.

His articles have been published in *Forbes, TechCrunch, MIT Technology Review,* and *Huffington Post.* His educational background includes a B.Engg (Electronics) and MBA (Finance and Marketing) from the University of Pune, India.

About the Website

A book is static and a website is anything but static. At this books digital dynamic twin - www.theresilientfounder.org, you will find new research, data, anecdotes, and quotes. Founders can find strength, solace, community, and support as they find their way out of dark nights.

Here, we can share their stories for the benefit of one and all. The site contents follow the overall book structure:

- Managing our psychology
- Therapy – what works and what does not
- Managing our recovery
- Supporting and caring for the depressed

While this outline is a starting point, the structure stays flexible. Please email me at mr@theresilientfounder.org with any suggestions. We live, learn, and support each other as we progress.

Index

Page numbers followed by *f* and *t* refer to figures and tables, respectively.